IMPROVING
YOUR SERVE

Books by Charles R. Swindoll:

Come Before Winter
Compassion: Showing Care in a Careless World
Dropping Your Guard
Encourage Me
For Those Who Hurt
Growing Deep in the Christian Life
Growing Strong in the Seasons of Life
Growing Wise in Family Life
Hand Me Another Brick
Improving Your Serve
Killing Giants, Pulling Thorns
Leadership: Influence That Inspires
Living Above the Level of Mediocrity
Living Beyond the Daily Grind I, II
Living on the Ragged Edge
Make Up Your Mind
The Quest for Character
Recovery: When Healing Takes Time
Standing Out
Starting Over
Strengthening Your Grip
Strike the Original Match
Three Steps Forward, Two Steps Back
Victory: A Winning Game Plan for Life
You and Your Child

Booklets by Charles R. Swindoll:

Anger
Attitudes
Commitment
Dealing with Defiance
Demonism
Destiny
Divorce
Eternal Security
God's Will
Hope
Impossibilities
Integrity
Leisure
The Lonely Whine of the Top Dog
Moral Purity
Our Mediator
Peace in Spite of Panic
Prayer
Sensuality
Singleness
Stress
Tongues
When Your Comfort Zone Gets the Squeeze
Woman

CHARLES R. SWINDOLL

IMPROVING YOUR·SERVE

WORD PUBLISHING

Dallas·London·Vancouver·Melbourne

IMPROVING YOUR SERVE: THE ART OF UNSELFISH LIVING

Copyright © 1981 by Word, Incorporated, Waco, Texas 76796
ISBN 0-8499-0267-3 (regular edition)
ISBN 0-8499-3851-1 (deluxe edition)
ISBN 0-8499-3214-9 (paperback edition)
Library of Congress catalog card number: 80-54553
Printed in the United States of America

Unless otherwise indicated, Scripture quotations are from *The New American Standard Bible,* copyright 1960, 1962, 1963, 1968, 1971, 1972, 1973, 1975, by the Lockman Foundation and used by permission.

Scripture quotations identified TLB are from *The Living Bible Paraphrased* (Wheaton: Tyndale House Publishers, 1971).

Scripture quotations identified NIV are from the Holy Bible: New International Version, copyright © 1978 by the New York International Bible Society. Used by permission of Zondervan Bible Publishers.

Scripture quotations identified PHILLIPS are from *The New Testament in Modern English,* copyright © 1958, 1960, 1972 by J. B. Phillips.

Scripture quotations identified NEB are from *The New English Bible,* © 1961, 1970 The Delegates of the Oxford University Press and The Syndics of the Cambridge University Press.

Scripture quotations identified KJV are from the King James Version of the Bible.

The quotation on pages 94-95 is reprinted with permission of Macmillan Publishing Co., Inc., from *Creative Brooding* by Robert Raines. Copyright © 1966 by Robert Raines.

3 4 5 6 7 8 9 LBM 11 10 9 8

With much appreciation this book is dedicated to

HELEN AND BEVERLY PETERS

A mother-daughter team whose serve could hardly be improved.

Because of their efficient and unselfish assistance behind
the scenes, my wife and I have laughed more and worried less.

Contents

Introduction

For over two years I have been intrigued with a verse of Scripture found in Mark's account of the life of Jesus. At times this verse has haunted and convicted me. On other occasions I have been encouraged by it. When I have used it as a basis for evaluating leadership, I have usually been both surprised and shocked. More often than not, the truth of the verse in daily living is conspicuous by its absence. And among those we would expect to see it best displayed—the Christian community—it is not uncommon to find it seldom demonstrated.

The verse? Mark 10:45:

> For even the Son of Man did not come to be served, but to serve, and to give his life a ransom for many (NIV).

The truth? Authentic servanthood.

Read the verse again, this time aloud. When Jesus took the time to explain His reason for coming among us, He was simple and direct: to serve and to give. Not to *be* served. Not to grab the spotlight in the center ring. Not to make a name or attract attention or become successful or famous or powerful or idolized. No, quite frankly, that stuff turned Him off. The first-century world was full and running over with strong-willed dogmatists. Authority figures were a dime a dozen (they always are). There were Caesars and Herods and governors and other pompous hotshots in abundance. Some, like the Pharisees and Sadducees and scribes—people with whom Jesus locked horns from the earliest days of his ministry—even used religion as their lever to control others. But servants? I mean the authentic types who genuinely gave of themselves without concern over who got the glory? They were not to be found!

But before we cluck our tongues and wag our heads at those down the time tunnel, criticizing the Roman world for its conceit and arrogance, the fact is we've got some homework to catch up on in the 1980s. It was the startling realization of this over two years ago that forced me to stop in my tracks and do some serious thinking about servanthood. It's not that I'd never heard the word or tossed it around from time to time . . . but I honestly had not made a conscious effort to examine the concept of serving, either in Scripture or in its everyday outworking. I certainly had not been much of a model of it, I openly admit to my own embarrassment. Frankly, it is still a struggle. Serving and giving don't come naturally. Living an unselfish life is an art!

The result of my two-year pursuit has been more beneficial than words can describe. The finger of God's Spirit pointed me from one biblical passage to another. He then provided me perception in interpretation beyond my own ability and ultimately assisted me in appropriating and applying the principles that emerged from the pages of His Book. With remarkable regularity the Lord turned on the lights in areas that had been obscure or dark in my thinking throughout my Christian life. Big boulders that had blocked my vision and progress were shoved aside. Insight began to replace ignorance. Becoming a servant began to be something beautiful, yes, *essential*, rather than something fearful and weird. I not only desired it for myself (a process that is still going on), but I wanted to share with others what God was revealing to me.

I did just that. Sunday after Sunday I preached my heart out among the most teachable and responsive congregation a pastor could possibly enjoy. The series grew and multiplied from the pulpit at the First Evangelical Free Church of Fullerton, California, to our radio friends around the world who hear our broadcasts day after day on "Insight for Living." I have also spoken on the subject at Christian colleges, seminaries, banquets, and other gatherings in churches, radio rallies, and Christian conferences. Almost without exception those who have heard these messages have encouraged me to write a book that conveys this material in printed form.

While I was wrestling with this decision, Floyd Thatcher, vice president and editorial director of Word Books, expressed a keen interest in the subject and invited me to publish these chapters you are about to read. I freely express my gratitude to Floyd for both his vision and determination to make the dream become a reality. His contagious enthusiasm was like flint, continually prompting that spark I needed to stay at the task of putting my thoughts into print.

And to you, the reader, I will add just one final comment. This is a book to be applied. You don't have to be brilliant or gifted to pull off these truths in your life. *But you do have to be willing.* Before the ink on these pages can be permanently transferred to a change, first in your thinking and then in your living, there must be a willing spirit that says, "Lord, show me . . . teach me . . . help me . . . to serve and to give." If you will let that be your attitude, the process involved in your becoming more like Christ Himself will be much smoother, much faster, and much less painful.

Charles R. Swindoll
Fullerton, California

1

Who, Me a Servant? You Gotta Be Kidding!

The original idea of becoming a servant seemed either wrong or weird to me. I realize now I rejected it because my concept of a servant was somewhere between an African slave named Kunta Kinte straight out of *Roots* and those thousands of nameless migrant workers who, at harvest time, populate the farmlands and orchards across America. Both represented ignorance, objects of mistreatment, a gross absence of human dignity, and the epitome of many of the things Christianity opposes.

The mental image turned me off completely. Washing around in my head was a caricature of a pathetic creature virtually without will or purpose in life . . . bent over, crushed in spirit, lacking self-esteem, soiled, wrinkled, and weary. You know, sort of a human mule who, with a sigh, shuffles and trudges down the long rows of life. Don't ask me why, but that was my perception every time I heard the word *servant*. Candidly, the idea disgusted me.

And confusion was added to my disgust when I heard people

(especially preachers) link the two terms *servant* and *leader*. They seemed as opposite as light and dark, a classic example of the proverbial round peg in a square hole. I distinctly remember thinking back then, "Who, *me* a servant! You gotta be kidding!"

Perhaps that's your initial reaction, too. If so, I understand. But you're in for a pleasant surprise. I have great news based on some very helpful information that will—if applied—change your mind and then your life. It excites me when I consider how God is going to use these words in this book to introduce to you (as He did to me) the truth concerning authentic servanthood. How desperately we need to improve our serve!

Several years ago I read of a fascinating experiment conducted by the National Institute of Mental Health. It took place in a nine-foot square cage designed to house, comfortably, 160 mice. For two and a half years, the colony of mice grew from 8 to 2200. Plenty of food, water, and other resources were continually provided. All mortality factors (except aging) were eliminated. Dr. John Calhoun, a research psychologist, began to witness a series of unusual phenomena among the mice as the population reached its peak. Within the cage, from which the mice could not escape, the colony began to disintegrate.

· Adults formed groups or cliques of about a dozen mice in each group.

· In these groups, different mice performed particular social functions.

· The males who normally protected their territory withdrew from leadership and became uncharacteristically passive.

· The females became unusually aggressive and forced out the young.

· The young found themselves without a place in the society, and they grew to be increasingly more self-indulgent. They ate, drank, slept, and groomed themselves, but showed no normal assertiveness.

· The whole "mouse society" ultimately became disrupted . . . and after five years *all the mice had died,* even though there was an abundance of food, water, resources, and an absence of disease.

What was most interesting to the observers was the strong independence, the extreme isolation syndrome of the mice. This was greatly emphasized by the fact that courtship and mating—the most complex activities for mice—were the first activities to cease.

What result would similar conditions have on humanity? What would be the results of overcrowded conditions on an inescapable planet with all the accompanying stress factors? Dr. Calhoun suggested that we would first of all cease to reproduce our ideas, and along with ideas, our goals, ideals, and values would be lost.[1]

It's happening.

Our world has become a large, impersonal, busy institution. We are alienated from each other. Although crowded, we are lonely. Distant. Pushed together but uninvolved. No longer do most neighbors visit across the backyard fence. The well-manicured front lawn is the modern moat that keeps barbarians at bay. Hoarding and flaunting have replaced sharing and caring. It's like we are occupying common space but have no common interests, as if we're on an elevator with rules like: "No talking, smiling, or eye contact allowed without written consent of the management."

Painful though it may be for us to admit it here in this great land of America, we're losing touch with one another. The motivation to help, to encourage, yes, to *serve* our fellow-man is waning. People have observed a crime in progress but refused to help so as not to be involved. Even our foundational values are getting lost in these confusing days. And yet, it is these things that form the essentials of a happy and fulfilled life.

Remember that grand declaration of biblical assurance etched in the rocklike truth of Romans 8? I'm referring to verses 28–29, which read:

> And we know that God causes all things to work together for good to those who love God, to those who are called according to His purpose.
> For whom He foreknew, He also predestined to become

conformed to the image of His Son, that He might be the first-born among many brethren.

Maybe you've never before stopped to consider that God is committed to *one* major objective in the lives of all His people: to conform us to "the image of His Son." We need to blow the dust off that timeless goal now that our cage is overcrowded and our lives are growing increasingly more distant from each other.

Exactly what does our heavenly Father want to develop within us? What is that "image of His Son"? Well, rather than getting neck deep in tricky theological waters, I believe the simple answer is found in Christ's own words. Listen as He declares His primary reason for coming:

> For even the Son of Man did not come to be served, but to serve, and to give His life a ransom for many (Mark 10:45).

No mumbo jumbo. Just a straight-from-the-shoulder admission. He came to serve and to give. It makes sense, then, to say that God desires the same for us. After bringing us into His family through faith in His Son, the Lord God sets His sights on building into us the same quality that made Jesus distinct from all others in His day. He is engaged in building into His people the same serving and giving qualities that characterized His Son.

Nothing is more refreshing than a servant's heart and a giving spirit, especially when we see them displayed in a person many would tag as a celebrity. A couple of years ago my wife and I attended the National Religious Broadcasters convention in Washington, D.C., where one of the main speakers was Colonel James B. Irwin, former astronaut who was a part of the crew that had made the successful moon walk. He spoke of the thrill connected with leaving this planet and seeing it shrink in size. He mentioned watching earthrise one day . . . and thinking how privileged he was to be a member of that unique crew. And then he began to realize en route back home that many would consider him a "superstar," for sure an international celebrity.

Humbled by the awesome goodness of God, Colonel Irwin shared his true feelings, which went something like this:

As I was returning to earth, I realized that I was a servant—not a celebrity. So I am here as God's servant on planet Earth to share what I have experienced that others might know the glory of God.

God allowed this man to break loose from the small cage we call "Earth," during which time He revealed to him a basic motto all of us would do well to learn: *a servant, not a celebrity.* Caught up in the fast-lane treadmill of Century Twenty— making mad dashes through airports, meeting deadlines, being responsible for big-time decisions, and coping with the stress of people's demands mixed with our own high expectations—it's easy to lose sight of our primary calling as Christians, isn't it? Even the busy mother of small children struggles with this. Mounds of ironing and the endless needs of her husband and kids block out the big picture.

If you're like me, you sometimes think, "I would give anything to be able to step back into the time when Jesus cast His shadow on earth. How great it must have been to sit back as one of the Twelve and soak up all those truths He taught. I mean, *they must have really learned how to serve, to give of themselves."* Right? Wrong!

Allow me to journey back with you to one of the many scenes that demonstrated just how typical those guys really were. I'm referring to an occasion when our Lord's popularity was on the rise . . . the knowledge of His kingdom was spreading . . . and the disciples began to be anxious about being recognized as members of His chosen band.

What makes this account a bit more interesting is the presence of a *mother* of two of the disciples. She's Mrs. Zebedee, wife of the Galilean fisherman and mother of James and John. Let's consider her request:

Then the mother of the sons of Zebedee came to Him with her sons, bowing down, and making a request of Him.

And He said to her, "What do you wish?" She said to Him, "Command that in Your kingdom these two sons of mine may sit, one on Your right and one on Your left" (Matt. 20:20–21).

Now don't be too tough on this dear Jewish mother. She's proud of her sons! She had thought about that request for quite some time. Her motive was probably pure and her idea was in proper perspective. She didn't ask that her sons occupy the center throne, of course not—that belonged to Jesus. But like any good mother who watches out for "breaks in life" that could lead to a nice promotion, she pushed for James and John as candidates for thrones number two and number three. She wanted to enhance their image before the public. She wanted people to think highly of her boys who had left their nets and entered this up-and-coming ministry. They were among "the Twelve."

And that needed recognition!

Just in case you're wondering how the other ten felt about this, check out verse 24. It says "the ten became indignant." Guess why. Hey, no way were they going to give up those top spots without a fight. They got downright ticked off that maybe James and John might get the glory they wanted. Sound familiar?

With biting conviction Jesus answers the mother with this penetrating comment: "You do not know what you are asking for . . ." (v. 22). That must have stung. She really thought she did. Enamored of her world of soldiers with medals, emperors with jeweled crowns, governors with slaves awaiting their every need, and even merchants with their employees . . . it seemed only fitting for those two sons of hers to have thrones, especially if they were charter members of the God movement, soon to be a "kingdom." Rulers need thrones!

No. This movement is different. Jesus pulls His disciples aside and spells out the sharp contrast between His philosophy and the world system in which they lived. Read His words slowly and carefully.

> But Jesus called them to Himself, and said, "You know that the rulers of the Gentiles lord it over them, and their great men exercise authority over them.
>
> "It is not so among you, but whoever wishes to become great

among you shall be your servant, and whoever wishes to be first among you shall be your slave; just as the Son of Man did not come to be served, but to serve, and to give His life a ransom for many" (Matt. 20:25–28).

In the secular system there are distinct levels of authority. It's true today, for sure. In government there is our president, his cabinet, and a large body of personally selected men who have privileges the common citizen does not possess. In the military there are officers and enlisted men . . . and ranks within each. In sports there are coaches and players. In the business world there are corporation heads and lines of authority between managers and personnel, shop superintendents, foremen, and laborers. The person in the labor force is expected to punch a clock, show up on time, work hard, and not take advantage of his or her employer. There's a name for those who choose not to follow those directions. Unemployed! Why? Because the boss is in charge. That's the way the system works. As Jesus put it, "their great men exercise authority over them." But then he adds, "It is *not so* among you" (emphasis added). What isn't so? Simply this, in God's family there is to be one great body of people: servants. In fact, that's the way to the top in His kingdom.

> . . . whoever wishes to become great among you shall be your servant.

Forgotten words.

Yes, these seem to be forgotten words, even in many churches with their smooth pastors, high powered executives, and superstar singers. Unfortunately, there doesn't seem to be much of the servant mentality in such settings. Even in our church life we tend to get so caught up in a success and size race that we lose sight of our primary calling as followers of Christ. The "celebrity syndrome" so present in our Christian thought and activities just doesn't square with the attitudes and messages of Jesus. We have skidded into a pattern whereby the celebrities and top dogs in our church life call the shots, and it is difficult to be a servant when you're used to telling others what to do.

Maybe I need to clarify what I mean. In the Body of Christ there is one Head. Christ Jesus is Lord of His body.

> And He is the image of the invisible God, the first-born of all creation.
>
> For in Him all things were created, both in the heavens and on earth, visible and invisible, whether thrones or dominions or rulers or authorities—all things have been created through Him and for Him.
>
> And He is before all things, and in Him all things hold together.
>
> He is also head of the body, the church; and He is the beginning, the first-born from the dead; so that He Himself might come to have first place in everything (Col. 1:15–18).

No human being dare take that position. A man named Diotrephes, mentioned in John's third letter, verses 9 and 10, attempted to do so and was openly rebuked by the apostle. Diotrephes becomes a warning to anyone who desires to become the "church boss." It may be a board member, a pastor, a teacher, a musician, a *former* officer or pastor in a church. No matter who, the Diotrephes mentality has no place in the Body. Only Christ is the Head. All the rest of us are in the class Jesus spoke of in Matthew 20 . . . *servants.*

You're probably saying, "But there must be leadership to get the job done." Yes, I agree. But it must be servant-hearted leadership among *all.* You see, I am not interested in which form of government you or your church may embrace, but only that every one involved in that ministry (whether leader or not) sees himself as one who serves, one who gives. It's the *attitude* that is most important.

Perhaps the finest model, except Christ Himself, was that young Jew from Tarsus who was radically transformed from a strong-willed official in Judaism to a bond servant of Jesus Christ—Paul. What a remarkable change, what a remarkable man!

It's possible you have the notion that the apostle Paul rammed his way through life like a fully loaded battleship at sea. Blasting and pounding toward objectives, he was just too important to worry about the little people or those who got in his way. After all, *he was Paul!* I must confess that is not too far removed from my original impression of the man in my earlier years as a Christian. He was, in my mind, the blend of a Christian John Wayne, Clint Eastwood, and the Hulk. I mean, he got things done.

But that false impression began to fade when I made an in-depth study of Paul—his style, his own self-description, even his comments to various churches and people as he wrote to each. I discovered that the man I had thought was the prima donna *par excellence* considered himself quite the contrary. Almost without exception he begins every piece of correspondence with words to this effect: "Paul, a servant . . ." or "Paul, a bond-slave. . . ."

The more I pondered those words, the deeper they penetrated. This man, the one who certainly could have expected preferential treatment or demanded a high-and-mighty role of authority over others, referred to himself most often as a "servant" of God. Amazing. He was indeed an apostle, but he conducted himself, he carried himself, as a servant. I found this extremely appealing.

The longer I thought about this concept, the more evidence emerged from the Scripture to support it. In fact, most of the discoveries fell into one of three categories of characteristics related to this servant image—*transparent humanity, genuine humility, absolute honesty.*

Transparent Humanity

Listen to Paul's words to the Corinthians:

And when I came to you, brethren, I did not come with superiority of speech or of wisdom, proclaiming to you the testimony of God. For I determined to know nothing among you except Jesus Christ, and Him crucified. And I was with you in weakness and in fear and in much trembling (1 Cor. 2:1–3).

"Aw, the guy is just being modest," you answer. No, not when you compare these words with the popular opinion of him:

. . . "His letters are weighty and strong, but his personal presence is unimpressive, and his speech contemptible" (2 Cor. 10:10).

That's quite a shock. The man didn't have it all together—he wasn't perfect—and (best of all) he didn't attempt to hide it! He admitted to his friends in Corinth he was weak, fearful, and even trembling when he stood before them. I admire such transparency. Everybody does if it's the truth.

I forget where I found the following statement, but it's been in my possession for years. It vividly describes Paul as being ". . . a man of moderate stature with curly hair and scanty, crooked legs, protruding eyeballs, large knit eyebrows, a long nose, and thick lips."

Wow! Certainly doesn't sound like any one of the many smooth public idols of our day. And we know for a fact he suffered terribly from poor eyesight (Gal. 6:11), plus some are convinced the man had a hunchback.

Without hiding a bit of his humanity (see Romans 7 if you still struggle believing he was a cut above human), Paul openly declares his true condition. He had needs and admitted them. Servants do that. He didn't have everything in life wired perfectly . . . and he didn't hide it. Servants are like that. Immediately you can begin to see some of the comforting aspects of having a servant's heart. Paul admitted his humanity.

That brings us to the second characteristic of servants.

Genuine Humility

Going back for a moment to that first Corinthian letter, Paul also admits:

And my message and my preaching were not in persuasive words of wisdom, but in demonstration of the Spirit and of power, that your faith should not rest on the wisdom of men, but on the power of God (1 Cor. 2:4–5).

Now for a preacher, that's quite a comment. The man comes up front and declares not only his lack of persuasiveness, but his reason why—that they might not be impressed with *his* ability, but rather with *God's* power. There's something very authentic in Paul's humility. Over and over we read similar words in his writings. I'm convinced that those who were instructed, face to face, by the man became increasingly more impressed with the living Christ and less impressed with him.

When people follow image-conscious leaders, the leader is exalted. He is placed on a pedestal and ultimately takes the place of the Head of the church.

When people follow leaders with servant hearts, the Lord God is exalted. Those people speak of God's person, God's power, God's work, God's name, God's Word . . . all for God's glory. Let me suggest a couple of revealing tests of humility:

1. *A nondefensive spirit when confronted.* This reveals a willingness to be accountable. Genuine humility operates on a rather simple philosophy:

Nothing to prove
Nothing to lose.

2. *An authentic desire to help others.* I'm referring to a sensitive, spontaneous awareness of needs. A true servant stays in touch with the struggles others experience. There is that humility of mind that continually looks for ways to serve and to give.

ABSOLUTE HONESTY

Finally, let's think about another mark of servanthood: integrity (absolute honesty).

Remember these words?

> Therefore since we have this ministry, as we received mercy, we do not lose heart, but we have renounced the things hidden because of shame, not walking in craftiness or adulterating the word of God, but by the manifestation of truth commending ourselves to every man's conscience in the sight of God (2 Cor. 4:1–2).

And how about these?

> For our exhortation does not come from error or impurity or by way of deceit; but just as we have been approved by God to be entrusted with the gospel, so we speak, not as pleasing men but God, who examines our hearts (1 Thess. 2:3–4).

There really isn't much to add. Honesty has a beautiful and refreshing simplicity about it . . . as do servants of God. No ulterior motives. No hidden meanings. An absence of hypocrisy, duplicity, political games, and verbal superficiality. As honesty and real integrity characterize our lives, there will be no need to manipulate others. We'll come to the place where all the substitutes will turn us off once we cultivate a taste for the genuine, the real.

I'm far from through, but this is enough for one sitting. We need to put it on the back burner and let it simmer for awhile. Before going on into the next chapter, take time to give some thought to your own life. Think about becoming more of a servant . . . think of things like transparent humanity and genuine humility and absolute honesty. Being real, that's the major message of this chapter—being who you really are—and then allowing the Lord God to develop within you a style of serving that fits you.

Some time ago I stumbled across a book for children that contained a message for adults. The main character in the book is a little stuffed rabbit, all shiny and new, who goes through the process of becoming "real," that is, more than just a toy on a shelf. As he struggles with those initial feelings of uneasiness (as perhaps you are struggling with the concept of servanthood), he engages an old, worn-out, well-used, much-loved stuffed horse in conversation. Because the dialogue between the two says so clearly what I've been trying to say in this chapter, it is a conclusion that is both appropriate and needed.

The Skin Horse had lived longer in the nursery than any of the others. He was so old that his brown coat was bald in patches and showed the seams underneath, and most of the hairs in his tail had been pulled out to string bead necklaces. He was wise, for he had seen a long succession of mechanical toys arrive to boast and swagger, and by-and-by break their mainsprings and pass away, and he knew that they were only toys, and would never turn into anything else. For nursery magic is very strange and wonderful, and only those playthings that are old and wise and experienced like the Skin Horse understand all about it.

"What is REAL?" asked the Rabbit one day, when they were lying side by side near the nursery fender, before Nana came to tidy the room. "Does it mean having things that buzz inside you and a stick-out handle?"

"Real isn't how you are made," said the Skin Horse. "It's a thing that happens to you. When a child loves you for a long, long time, not just to play with, but REALLY loves you, then you become real."

"Does it hurt?" asked the Rabbit.

"Sometimes," said the Skin Horse, for he was always truthful. "When you are Real you don't mind being hurt."

"Does it happen all at once, like being wound up," he asked, "or bit by bit?"

"It doesn't happen all at once," said the Skin Horse. "You become. It takes a long time. That's why it doesn't often happen to people who break easily, or have sharp edges, or who have to be carefully kept. Generally, by the time you are Real, most of your hair has been loved off, and your eyes drop out and you get loose in the joints and very shabby. But these things don't matter at all, because once you are real you can't be ugly, except to people who don't understand."[2]

2

A Case for Unselfishness

I
ME
MINE
MYSELF

Those four words stood out in bold print. They appeared as if they were forming an enormous monument, each letter seemingly chiseled out of granite. At the base of this strange "monument" were hundreds, perhaps thousands, of people with their arms held up high, as if worshiping at a shrine. And then in very small letters, this caption appeared at the bottom of the editorial cartoon: "Speaking of American cults . . ."

Surrounding the borders of this picture were four familiar lines from well-known commercials:

"Have it your way."

"Do yourself a favor."

"You owe it to yourself."

"You deserve a break today."[1]

Jab, jab. Twist, twist. That kind of stuff *really* hurts. Because it is so terribly true. Yet, we constantly applaud the I-me-mine-myself philosophy in subtle as well as overt ways. We make books on the subject of selfishness bestsellers by buying them by the millions. We put the gifted on a pedestal and secretly (if not publicly) worship at their shrine. And we make every effort to "look out for number one" at all cost. Let's admit it, ours is an age of gross selfishness. The "me" era. And we get mighty uncomfortable even when God begins to make demands on us. After all, this business of wholesale commitment to the cause of Christ needs to be kept in proper bounds!

Laced with similar tones of sarcasm are the words of Wilbur Rees:

> I would like to buy $3 worth of God, please, not enough to explode my soul or disturb my sleep, but just enough to equal a cup of warm milk or a snooze in the sunshine. I don't want enough of Him to make me love a black man or pick beets with a migrant. I want ecstasy, not transformation; I want the warmth of the womb, not a new birth. I want a pound of the Eternal in a paper sack. I would like to buy $3 worth of God, please.[2]

That's it. Our inner "self" doesn't want to dump God entirely, just keep Him at a comfortable distance. Three dollars of Him is sufficient. A sack full, nothing more. Just enough to keep my guilt level below the threshold of pain, just enough to guarantee escape from eternal flames. But certainly not enough to make me nervous . . . to start pushing around my prejudices or nit-picking at my lifestyle. *Enough is enough!*

A Proper Perspective

Now before we get too carried away, a couple of statements need to be made to clarify the issue. First, a good self-esteem is not the same as selfishness. Without a strong belief in ourselves, we are easily crippled and wounded in life. A poor self-image is not to be equated with humility or the mark of a servant. As a matter of fact, without a healthy ego, without the confidence that God is in us, on our side, pulling for us, we become fragile, easily bruised, counterproductive people.

I like what Mrs. Chuck Noll said about her husband, the coach of the Pittsburgh Steelers: "He's got a very sturdy ego, but as for vanity—absolutely none."[3]

Let's not confuse a strong, sturdy self-esteem with vain selfishness. They are not twins, by any means.

Second, becoming a Christian does not automatically erase the presence of selfishness. It helps, of course, but it isn't a cure-all. We Christians must still fight the battle of pride. We evangelicals tend to be exclusive and snobbish rather than broad-minded and accepting. We are proud that we have the answers while others don't. We'd never come right out and call it pride, but deep down inside we feel rather smug with our charts and diagrams of complex theological issues. It's easy to look down our noses at those who aren't as informed as we.

A Biblical Basis

It's been my experience that before I can fully conquer any problem, I need to understand it as well as possible, especially its origin. To do that with "self" we must go back, way back, to that ancient scene pictured for us in the second and third chapters of Genesis, the Garden of Eden. What a super spot! Beautiful beyond description, a perfect, pollution-free atmosphere, luxurious foliage, fragant flowers, crystal-clear water—that garden would make Tahiti look like a pigsty by comparison. And on top of all the physical beauty, there was absolute innocence. No sin. Which means that Adam and Eve had a relationship that was free of hang-ups. The last verse in Genesis 2 verifies that: "And the man and his wife were both naked and were not ashamed."

Naked. Laid bare, open. Not just physically, but emotionally as well. That explains why they were not ashamed. The Hebrew construction suggests they were not ashamed "with one another." There was this remarkable openness, a lack of self-consciousness in each other's presence. Talk about the ideal marriage! Their discussions, their actions, their entire existence were nondefensive, unguarded, and absolutely unselfish.

How could it be? No sin. Therefore, no selfishness. Until . . .

You guessed it. Enter the devil with his alluring offer (read Gen. 3:1–6) and exit innocence with its pleasurable benefits. And the result?

> Then the eyes of both of them were opened, and they knew that they were naked; and they sewed fig leaves together and made themselves loin coverings (3:7).

Don't miss what that says about their eyes. They were *opened*. There was a sudden, shocking realization they were naked. Seems amazing to us, doesn't it? You and I couldn't be more aware of those times when we are naked. Just a half-opened zipper makes us blush.

But remember the difference. Suddenly, those two became *self*-conscious. They'd never known those feelings before. You and I have never known anything else. What we read here in the Genesis account is the origin of self-awareness, self-concern, selfishness. If you read on you'll see that they immediately began to look out for number one.

> And they heard the sound of the Lord God walking in the garden in the cool of the day, and the man and his wife hid themselves from the presence of the Lord God among the trees of the garden (3:8).

Adam didn't assist Eve. She really wasn't concerned about him either. Both got busy and whipped up a self-made cover-up. And (can you believe it) they attempted to hide from the Lord God. Of course, you can believe it! To this day it's mankind's favorite game . . . even though we lose every time we play it.

> Then the Lord God called to the man, and said to him, "Where are you?"
>
> And he said, "I heard the sound of Thee in the garden, and I was afraid because I was naked; so I hid myself" (3:9–10).

J. Grant Howard does a splendid job of describing the inner turmoil of these two in the garden. Notice they've already started wearing masks.

> Forced out of hiding. Adam stands shamefacedly before his Judge and mumbles his reply. These are the first recorded words of a sinner. Note how he communicates. He mixes truth—"I was afraid"—with half-truth—"because I was naked." The full truth was that he had disobeyed God and thus was aware of his nakedness. He did not level with God. He concealed his act of willful disobedience instead of openly and honestly confessing it. Adam can no longer function as a complete authentic person.[4]

As God probed deeper, Adam and Eve became increasingly more defensive. They hurled accusations at each other and then at God.

"The woman. . . !"

"The woman *you* gave me. . . !"

"The serpent. . . ."

The pattern hasn't changed, has it? Since the original scene down through the centuries, the history of humanity is smeared with ugly marks of selfishness. Unwilling to be authentic, we hide, we deny, we lie, we run, we escape. Anything but the whole truth!

And we hurl. We ridicule, we dominate, we criticize. We cut a person to ribbons with our words. And then we develop ways to keep from admitting it.

"I'm not dogmatic, I'm just sure of myself."

"I'm not judging, I'm discerning."

"I'm not argumentative, I'm simply trying to prove a point."

"I'm not stubborn, *just confident!*"

And all this comes pouring out of our mouths with hardly a second thought. And in case you live under the delusion that we are mild-mannered and gracious in getting our way, watch what happens in heavy traffic . . . or at the checkstand in the local grocery store. I mean, we go for the jugular!

A couple of summers ago my older son Curt and I took a few

days off together and shot the rapids up at the Rogue River in Oregon. We went with several of the men from our church. It was great! While we were receiving instructions from the guide (there were about fifteen in the entire group) I began to study the canoes with my eyes. Some were old and worn, but a few were new. Being selfish, I wanted Curt and me to get the new ones . . . so I whispered in his ear,

"Curt, start moving over to the left."

"Why?"

"Just do as I say, son. The two canoes on the end are new. Let's get 'em."

He cooperated. And we got two of the new ones. I handled it so smoothly, nobody even knew it. The older ones were just as good . . . but they were old.

And there was a really salty old pro as a guide plus a couple of rookies. Guess which one we got. Right! I manipulated our way so efficiently, we wound up in his group.

Why? Because I'm selfish, plain and simple. And to make matters worse, I was *discipling my son to be selfish too!* In a couple of more years he will have it down pat.

By the way, on the way back to our campsite at the end of the day, all fifteen of us were packed like sardines in this old van. Everybody was dog tired. All of a sudden BOOM! A blowout on the right rear. All our gear had to come out to get to the spare tire. And then that beast of a van had to be jacked up. It was a hot, dirty job. Guess who directed traffic instead of helping to change the tire. As I recall not one car passed us on that country road during the entire episode.

Now, let me tell you the worst part of all, and it's really with embarrassment I do so. It was not until the next day that it dawned me that I was being selfish in any of this. Talk about a blind spot! You see, I learned a lot about looking out for *self* in school; I perfected it in the Marine Corps, and I developed ways to pull it off with real finesse in seminary, learning to be a minister. Hey, this is the profession where a guy can get away with it and hardly ever be criticized for it . . . even though we should! But who in the world is going to point a finger at a man of the cloth? Who's willing to touch "God's anointed" (our favorite title) and risk an advanced case of leprosy?

But my selfishness didn't start at school or in the Corps or at seminary, for that matter. I, like you, caught the disease from Adam. It's a congenital illness in all of us. No person has ever lived on this earth completely free of this dreaded plague—except One. That's right, ever since Adam, only God's virgin-born Son has had immunity from contamination with sin. He did no sin, knew no sin, had no sin. Being sinless, He lived like no other man ever lived. He spoke as no other man ever spoke. And as that unique Teacher, He cut a new swath. He gave directions that had never been given before by *any* instructor.

> . . . "You know that the rulers of the Gentiles lord it over them, and their great men exercise authority over them.
> "It is not so among you, but whoever wishes to become great among you shall be your servant, and whoever wishes to be the first among you shall be your slave; just as the Son of Man did not come to be served, but to serve, and to give His life a ransom for many" (Matt. 20:25–28).

We who are infected with the Adam-Eve disease don't operate like that. Not on your life. This was emphasized afresh as I watched Leonard Bernstein, the famous orchestra conductor, perform one evening on television. During an informal time of discussion on the program, I recall one admirer asked: "Mr. Bernstein, what is the most difficult instrument to play?" He responded with quick wit:

> Second fiddle. I can get plenty of first violinists, but to find one who plays *second* violin with as much enthusiasm or *second* French horn or *second* flute, now that's a problem. And yet if no one plays second, we have no harmony.

Wise words . . . and true!

That's one of the reasons Jesus Christ was so different. Not only did He encourage that sort of thing, He *modeled* it continually. On the basis of this, Paul could write:

Do nothing from selfishness or empty conceit, but with humility of mind let each of you regard one another as more important than himself; do not merely look out for your own personal interests but also for the interests of others.

Have this attitude in yourselves which was also in Christ Jesus (Phil. 2:3–5).

What different counsel we get from man! J. B. Phillips illustrates this when he alters the Beatitudes to read as follows:

Happy are the "pushers": for they get on in the world.

Happy are the hard-boiled: for they never let life hurt them.

Happy are they who complain: for they get their own way in the end.

Happy are the blasé: for they never worry over their sins.

Happy are the slavedrivers: for they get results.

Happy are the knowledgeable men of the world: for they know their way around.

Happy are the troublemakers: for they make people take notice of them.[5]

No, that is just the opposite of what our Lord originally said. In simplest terms, remember, He told us to serve and to give. In those words He built a case for unselfish living. Not being satisfied with just "three dollars worth of God." No, not for authentic servants . . . not on your life. But rather being willing to give it all up to Him, for His glory. This has been referred to as "buying the pearl of great price."

With a bit of sanctified imagination, one man offers this dialogue to illustrate just how much is involved in releasing our all to God so we are free to serve others:

"I want this pearl. How much is it?"

"Well," the seller says, "it's very expensive."

"But, how much?" we ask.

"Well, a very large amount."

"Do you think I could buy it?"

"Oh, of course, everyone can buy it."

"But, didn't you say it was very expensive?"

"Yes."

"Well, how much is it?"

"Everything you have," says the seller.

We make up our minds, "All right, I'll buy it," we say.

"Well, what do you have?" he wants to know. "Let's write it down."

"Well, I have ten thousand dollars in the bank."

"Good—ten thousand dollars. What else?"

"That's all. That's all I have."

"Nothing more?"

"Well, I have a few dollars here in my pocket."

"How much?"

We start digging. "Well, let's see—thirty, forty, sixty, eighty, a hundred, a hundred twenty dollars."

"That's fine. What else do you have?"

"Well, nothing. That's all."

"Where do you live?" He's still probing.

"In my house. Yes, I have a house."

"The house, too, then." He writes that down.

"You mean I have to live in my camper?"

"You have a camper? That, too. What else?"

"I'll have to sleep in my car!"

"You have a car?"

"Two of them."

"Both become mine, both cars. What else?"

"Well, you already have my money, my house, my camper, my cars. What more do you want?"

"Are you alone in this world?"

"No, I have a wife and two children. . . ."

"Oh, yes, your wife and children, too. What else?"

"I have nothing left! I am left alone now."

Suddenly the seller exclaims, "Oh, I almost forgot! You yourself, too! Everything becomes mine—wife, children, house, money, cars—and you too."

Then he goes on. "Now listen—I will allow you to use all these things for the time being. But don't forget that they are mine, just as you are. And whenever I need any of them you must give them up, because now I am the owner."[6]

That's what it means to come to terms with servanthood. Tough, tough concept, isn't it? Yes, tough . . . but now we know why.

Remember the monument?

I
ME
MINE
MYSELF

From now to the end of the book, we're going to assault that monument. We are going to give our full attention to what it means to be different.

Not a getter, but a giver.

Not one who holds a grudge, but a forgiver.

Not one who keeps score, but a forgetter.

Not a superstar, but a servant.

If you are ready to invest more than most . . . if you really desire more than three dollars worth of God, then read on. You're in for the time of your life.

3

The Servant As a Giver

I like the tongue-in-cheek definition of philosophers one of my Greek teachers in seminary would occasionally use. It's classic:

> Philosophers are people who talk about something they don't understand and make you think it's your fault![1]

Lots of philosophies are floating around, and most of them are more confusing than they are helpful. Interestingly, those that are clear enough to be understood usually end up focusing full attention on the individual. Consider a few of them:

Greece said, "Be wise, know yourself!"
Rome said, "Be strong, discipline yourself!"
Religion says, "Be good, conform yourself!"
Epicureanism says, "Be sensuous, enjoy yourself!"
Education says, "Be resourceful, expand yourself!"
Psychology says, "Be confident, assert yourself!"
Materialism says, "Be satisfied, please yourself!"

Pride says, "Be superior, promote yourself!"
Asceticism says, "Be lowly, suppress yourself!"
Humanism says, "Be capable, believe in yourself!"
Legalism says, "Be pious, limit yourself!"
Philanthropy says, "Be generous, release yourself!"

ISN'T THERE A BETTER WAY?

Yourself, yourself, yourself. We're up to here with self! Do something either *for* yourself or *with* yourself or *to* yourself. How very different from Jesus' model and message! No "philosophy" to turn our eyes inward, He offers rather a fresh and much-needed invitation to our "me-first" generation. There is a better way. Jesus says, "Be a servant, give to others!" Now that's a philosophy that anybody can understand. And, without question, it is attainable. Just listen:

> Do nothing from selfishness or empty conceit, but with humility of mind let each of you regard one another as more important than himself; do not merely look out for your own personal interests, but also for the interests of others (Phil. 2:3–4).

Know what all that means? Well, for starters, "nothing" means just that. Stop permitting two strong tendencies—selfishness and conceit—to control you! Let *nothing* either of them suggests win a hearing. Replace them with "humility of mind." But how? By regarding others as more important than yourself. Look for ways to support, encourage, build up, and stimulate the other person. And that requires an attitude that would rather give than receive.

"Humility of mind" is really an attitude, isn't it? It's a preset mentality that determines ahead of time thoughts like this:

· "I care about those around me."
· "Why do I always have to be first? I'm going to help someone else win for a change."

· "Today, it's my sincere desire to curb my own fierce competitive tendencies and turn that energy into encouraging at least one other person."

· "I willingly release my way this day. Lord, show me how You would respond to others, then make it happen in me."

Is All This Biblical?

Now before we get neck deep into this unselfish lifestyle, we need to determine if it is, in fact, promoted in Scripture. Does the Bible come right up front and encourage living like this? I'll let you determine the answer.

For the sake of space, let's limit our thoughts to just a few New Testament passages. Think as you read them slowly . . . and don't skip one line!

Be devoted to one another in brotherly love; give preference to one another in honor; not lagging behind in diligence, fervent in spirit, serving the Lord; rejoicing in hope, persevering in tribulation, devoted to prayer; contributing to the needs of the saints, practicing hospitality (Rom. 12:10–13).

For we do not preach ourselves but Christ Jesus as Lord, and ourselves as your bond-servants for Jesus' sake (2 Cor. 4:5).

For the love of Christ controls us, having concluded this, that one died for all, therefore all died; and He died for all, that they who live should no longer live for themselves, but for Him who died and rose again on their behalf (2 Cor. 5:14–15).

For you were called to freedom, brethren; only do not turn your freedom into an opportunity for the flesh, but through love serve one another (Gal. 5:13).

But we proved to be gentle among you, as a nursing mother tenderly cares for her own children.

Having thus a fond affection for you, we were well pleased to impart to you not only the gospel but also our own lives, because he had become very dear to us. . . .

Therefore encourage one another, and build up one another, just as you also are doing (1 Thess. 2:7–8; 5:11).

And let us consider how to stimulate one another to love and good deeds (Heb. 10:24).

And you will remember the section we looked at in chapter 1:

And I was with you in weakness and in fear and in trembling. And my message and my preaching were not in persuasive words of wisdom, but in demonstration of the Spirit and of power, that your faith should not rest on the wisdom of men, but on the power of God (1 Cor. 2:3–5).

Those words (there are many others) have a rare ring to them, don't they? In fact, some who read them might misunderstand and think I'm advocating inferiority. For your sake, a couple more biblical passages are needed:

For I consider myself not in the least inferior to the most eminent apostles. . . .
I have become foolish; you yourselves compelled me. Actually I should have been commended by you, for in no respect was I inferior to the most eminent apostles, even though I am a nobody (2 Cor. 11:5; 12:11).

There's the balance we're looking for. Authentic humility in no way should be confused with incompetence or lack of self-esteem. As a matter of fact, it is doubtful that anyone who wrestles with an unhealthy self-image can correctly and adequately give to others. Inferiority and unselfishness cannot coexist . . . not in the true sense, as Christ describes it.

What Are the Basics?

Now that we have laid a biblical foundation for servanthood, it is important to get some handles on what's involved in pulling it off. To get us started, let me suggest three basic ingredients:

giving, forgiving, and *forgetting.* Once you and I make up our minds to implement the truth of Philippians 2:3–4 (taking a special interest in others) or Galatians 5:13 (serving others in love), these three basics will begin to emerge. Instead of always thinking about receiving, we'll start looking for ways to give. Instead of holding grudges against those who offended us, we'll be anxious to forgive. And instead of keeping a record of what we've done or who we've helped, we'll take delight in forgetting the deed(s) and being virtually unnoticed. Our hunger for public recognition will diminish in significance.

In the next couple of chapters we'll think deeply about those last two, but for the balance of this chapter, let's picture the servant as a *giver* . . . one who quickly, willingly, and generously gives so others might benefit and grow.

How Should Servants Give?

Rather than jumping from one biblical reference to another, let's fix our attention on 2 Corinthians, chapter 8. This grand chapter of Scripture has an interesting background. Paul, the writer, is involved in collecting money for a hurting congregation in Jerusalem. As he makes his way through Europe, specifically the region of ancient Macedonia, he announces the need of those fellow Christians in Jerusalem. What adds to the significance of the whole episode is that Macedonia was already an economically depressed area. Macedonia was to Paul a lot like India is to us. It would be like encouraging the people of Appalachia to respond to those who are hurting in the ghetto of Harlem. "You people on welfare . . . give to those people on welfare!" would be a strange appeal today.

But the most remarkable fact of all is this: *They did!* Those financially deprived Macedonian believers were so concerned over their brothers and sisters in Jerusalem who did not have sufficient money to make ends meet, they *really* gave. Let's look closer and see just how extensively they did it.

Now, brethren, we wish to make known to you the grace of God which has been given in the churches of Macedonia, that in a great ordeal of affliction their abundance of joy and their deep poverty overflowed in the wealth of their liberality.

For I testify that according to their ability and beyond their ability they gave of their own accord, begging us with much entreaty for the favor of participation in the support of the saints, and this, not as we had expected, but they first gave themselves to the Lord and to us by the will of God (2 Cor. 8:1–5).

What a tremendous section of Scripture! I find several ways those Christians demonstrated authentic servanthood in their giving. When we give as a servant gives, the same things are true in us.

Anonymously

Not one specific church is mentioned, simply "the churches of Macedonia." Not even one individual is highlighted. No statues of bronze were later erected in Jerusalem, no names of super saints chiseled in marble or recorded in some book for others to ooh and ahh over. A great proof of true servanthood is *anonymity*.

One of my favorite poets, Ruth Harms Calkin, puts it well, entitling her thoughts, "I Wonder":

> You know, Lord, how I serve You
> With great emotional fervor
> In the limelight.
> You know how eagerly I speak for You
> At a women's club.
> You know how I effervesce when I promote
> A fellowship group.
> You know my genuine enthusiasm
> At a Bible study.
>
> But how would I react, I wonder
> If You pointed to a basin of water

> And asked me to wash the calloused feet
> Of a bent and wrinkled old woman
> Day after day
> Month after month
> In a room where nobody saw
> And nobody knew.[2]

Let those final words sink in, "nobody saw . . . nobody knew." When we practice the art of unselfish living, we prefer to remain anonymous. In fact, most of the people I know who possess a servant's heart are greatly embarrassed when their names are put up in lights.

Generously

Did you catch something else Paul said about those Macedonian servant-saints? When they gave, they "overflowed" in the process, they liberally and sacrificially gave "beyond their ability." I love the way he says that. Their giving dripped with sacrificial generosity. There wasn't a tightwad among them. How refreshing!

Now, as we apply this passage to the way true servants give, let's understand that the giving involved is much broader than money. That's for sure. It includes giving ourselves . . . our time and energy, our care and compassion, even our belongings on occasion. And what a need there is for this trait within the ranks of humanity today. And yet, how rare. We clutch our possessions so tightly we live most of our adult lives with white knuckles. I often wonder why. We certainly can't take any of it with us. I've never seen a hearse pulling a U-Haul!

The name of Onesiphorus flashes into my head. He's a guy who once modeled generosity in his giving to such an extent that Paul remembered his help while he was awaiting death. Listen to the apostle's remarks:

> The Lord grant mercy to the house of Onesiphorus for he often
> refreshed me, and was not ashamed of my chains; but when he
> was in Rome, he eagerly searched for me, and found me—the

Lord grant to him to find mercy from the Lord on that day—and you know very well what services he rendered at Ephesus (2 Tim. 1:16–18).

Did you miss a couple of choice, descriptive terms? Onesiphorus "often" refreshed the aging, imprisoned apostle, he "eagerly" stayed at the task of finding him. Those are words of great intensity, real determination, and eagerness. Paul's friend was a generous servant. He couldn't have cared less how much trouble it took to find him. He pursued!

Alexander Whyte, the insightful preacher of Edinburgh, Scotland, and writer of biographies, writes these moving words of Onesiphorus:

> Paul might be the greatest of the apostles to Onesiphorus, and he may be all that and far more than all that to you and to me, but he was only "Number so and so" to the soldier who was chained night and day to Paul's right hand. You would not have known Paul from any incognisable convict in our own penal settlements. Paul was simply "Number 5," or "Number 50," or "Number 500," or some such number. From one barrack-prison therefore to another Onesiphorus went about seeking for Paul day after day, week after week, often insulted, often threatened, often ill-used, often arrested and detained, till he was set free again only after great suffering and great expense. Till, at last, his arms were round Paul's neck, and the two old men were kissing one another and weeping to the amazement of all the prisoners who saw the scene. Noble-hearted Onesiphorus! We bow down before thee.[3]

Indeed, we do. Onesiphorus was the kind of servant we need more of: sacrificially generous. There is more.

Voluntarily

Back in 2 Corinthians 8, we're told that the Macedonians also gave voluntarily, not because somebody twisted their arms behind their backs. Paul writes:

. . . I can testify that they did it because they wanted to, and not because of nagging on my part. They begged us to take the money so they could share in the joy of helping . . . (2 Cor. 8:3–4, TLB).

A little later in that same letter, the apostle of grace encourages this spirit of voluntary spontaneity in our giving:

Let each one do just as he has purposed in his heart; not grudgingly or under compulsion; for God loves a cheerful giver (2 Cor. 9:7).

Sounds a lot like what Peter urges from pastors, elders, and other Christian leaders:

. . . shepherd the flock of God among you, not under compulsion, but voluntarily, according to the will of God; and not for sordid gain, but with eagerness; not yet as lording it over those allotted to your charge, but proving to be examples to the flock (1 Pet. 5:2–3).

Great counsel! If it is true that the best leaders are true servants (and I'm convinced that is correct), then one of the best ways to lead people into a willing spirit is to model it. That involves things like reaching out without being invited and sensing deep hurts without being told.

Marion Jacobsen, in a fine book entitled *Crowded Pews and Lonely People,* mentions a first-grader named Billy whose classmate Jim lost his father in a tractor accident. Billy prayed for Jim every day. One day as Billy was walking down the stairs at school, he saw Jim and decided to reach out to him.

"How are you getting along?"

"Oh, fine, jus' fine."

Bill continued, "Do you know, I've been praying for you ever since your daddy was killed."

The other little guy stopped and looked at Billy, grabbed his hand, and led him out back behind the school building. Then he opened up.

"You know, that was a lie when I said things are going fine; they aren't fine. We are having trouble with the cows and with the machines. My mother doesn't know what to do. But I didn't know you were praying for me."[4]

Just goes to show us, doesn't it, how many people are hurting, but don't feel free to say so until we voluntarily reach out to them.

Let's go back for a final glance at 2 Corinthians 8. There's one more characteristic we don't want to miss. The servants in Macedonia first gave *themselves* and then they gave their gifts.

Personally

This is a telltale sign of authentic servant-giving. It is impossible to give ourselves to others at arm's length or *in absentia*. Personal involvement is essential, not incidental, and it usually involves adapting our ways and schedules to fit into other's needs. Such personal involvement, however, certainly reveals the authenticity of our words.

Quite a while ago a young man I had known for several years expressed an interest in living in our home and being discipled in the context of our family. He assured me time and again, "I really want to help any way you or your wife may need me. My only reason for doing this is to serve. I just want to be a servant, Chuck."

Cynthia, the children, and I talked this over at length. We decided we'd give it a whirl . . . so in moved Mr. Servant and his family among our tribe of four kids, a dog, two hamsters, a rabbit, and a three-car garage full of stuff. It wasn't long before we realized those words, "I just want to be a servant" were mere words, little more. Time and again conflicts arose when our requests were met with his resistance. There was hardly an occasion when we would suggest that something be done a certain way without his offering an alternative suggestion. What began as an unselfish-sounding game plan (if I heard "I just want to be a servant" once I must have heard it fifty times) ultimately resulted in rather heated disagreements, much to our disappointment. Words come easy— but *being* a person who genuinely and personally gives to others calls for a plentiful supply of flexibility. There's much more to giving ourselves to the Lord and to others than making verbal statements.

According to these first five verses in 2 Corinthians 8, authentic servanthood calls for people with a passion for giving *whatever* without recognition, without reservation, without reluctance, and without restriction. And those types are rare indeed!

HOW MUCH DOES GIVING COST US?

Can you recall Jesus' radical philosophy I suggested at the beginning of this chapter? "Be a servant, give to others." The basis of that statement is tucked away in Luke 9:23:

> And He was saying to them all, "If anyone wishes to come after Me, let him deny himself, and take up his cross daily, and follow Me."

Following Christ as His disciple is a costly, unselfish decision. It calls for a radical examination of our self-centered lifestyles. Whew! That's another one of those easy things to say, but tough to carry out. Let's see if I can break this down into smaller bite-size chunks so we don't gag on it. When you look closely at Jesus' statement, a couple of things seem important. First, those who desire to follow Him closely must come to terms with *self-denial*. And second, this decision to give ourselves to others (taking up our cross) has to be a *daily* matter.

That's costly stuff. Terribly expensive.

If we read this back into the 2 Corinthians 8:1–5 guidelines regarding giving, and I really believe we should, then it isn't difficult to see some questions that we must ask and answer ourselves, like:

- Am I serious about being a close follower of Jesus Christ?
- Do I think of others to such an extent that self-denial is

becoming the rule rather than the exception in my life?
· Is my walk with Him a *daily* thing?

Making a Thorough Self-Evaluation

This takes us back to 2 Corinthians 8. After Paul finishes describing the unselfishness of the Macedonian believers (vv. 1–5), he turns to the Corinthians and exhorts them:

> But just as you abound in everything, in faith and utterance and knowledge and in all earnestness and in the love we inspired in you, see that you abound in this gracious work also.
> I am not speaking this as a command, but as proving through the earnestness of others the sincerity of your love also (2 Cor. 8:7–8).

A thorough self-evaluation is one of the requisites for following closely. The Corinthians *abounded* in vision, spiritual gifts, knowledge, zeal, and even love. Paul then says to abound in generosity too. Be givers! Be people who excel in *unselfishness!* This is timely advice for our own generation . . . and worth our thorough investigation.

It reminds me of an actual situation I heard about recently over the radio. A woman in West Palm Beach, Florida, died alone at the age of 71. The coroner's report was tragic. "Cause of death: *Malnutrition.*" The dear old lady wasted away to 50 pounds. Investigators who found her said the place where she lived was a veritable pigpen, the biggest mess you can imagine. One seasoned inspector declared he'd never seen a residence in greater disarray.

The woman had begged food at her neighbors' back doors and gotten what clothes she had from the Salvation Army. From all outward appearances she was a penniless recluse, a pitiful and forgotten widow. But such was not the case.

Amid the jumble of her unclean, disheveled belongings, two keys were found which led the officials to safe-deposit boxes at two different local banks. What they found was absolutely unbelievable.

The first contained over 700 AT&T stock certificates, plus hundreds of other valuable certificates, bonds, and solid financial securities . . . not to mention a stack of cash amounting to nearly $200,000. The second box had no certificates, only more currency—lots of it—$600,000 *to be exact*. Adding the net worth of both boxes, they found that the woman had in her possession well over A MILLION DOLLARS. Charles Osgood, reporting on CBS radio, announced that the estate would probably fall into the hands of a distant niece and nephew, neither of whom dreamed she had a thin dime to her name. She was, however, a millionaire who died a stark victim of starvation in a humble hovel many miles away.

I conducted a funeral several years ago for a man who died without family or friends. All he had was a fox terrier . . . to whom he left his entire estate: around $76,000.

We need to make an investigation of our own possessiveness, our tendency to hoard, to hold onto, rather than investing in the lives of others.

Sticking with a Commitment

There's another cost, equally exacting. As Paul continues with his instruction to the Corinthians, we see it clearly emerge:

> For you know the grace of our Lord Jesus Christ, that though He was rich, yet for your sake He became poor, that you through His poverty might become rich.
>
> And I give my opinion in this matter, for this is to your advantage, who were the first to begin a year ago not only to do this, but also to desire to do it.
>
> But now finish doing it also; that just as there was the readiness to desire it, so there may be also the completion of it by your ability (2 Cor. 8:9–11).

You see, a full year before he wrote them, they had begun that same project. No doubt they were filled with enthusiasm, the thrill of a fresh beginning. But in the passing of time, the newness had worn off. The spontaneous motivation to give had turned into a miserable marathon that dragged slowly on and on.

Paul says, "Get with it! You made a commitment to get involved, to give, and to help out—now stick with that commitment!"

Becoming a *giving* person sounds exciting. But it costs something. It will demand change, and no significant change ever got started without motivation and zeal.

Want a vivid illustration? Dieting. Oh, just the *word* brings up painful memories! Especially when I add exercising and jogging. Who hasn't had the experience? We finally get sick and tired of our flab. Zippers start ripping out, buttons pop off, the car leans dangerously to one side when we get in, the scales we step on punch out a little card that says, "Only one at a time, please."

We laugh understandingly at Erma Bombeck's continual battle with the bulge. You may remember she's the one who said something like, "I'm not telling you what I weigh, but when I measure my girth and then step on the scales, I oughta be a 90-foot redwood."

Okay, we're going to thin down. In the fresh enthusiasm of zeal, we buy $60 sneakers, a couple of $85 jogging outfits, we join a local spa (another $350), and we blow the dust off that miserable "Count Those Calories" booklet we bought back in the mid '70s. We are going to shave off 30 pounds!

The very first day we start with a flash. We hit the road, running like we're on fire. We drop our intake to 700 calories a day. We choke down dry toast, cottage cheese, sliced tomatoes, and boiled egg! We snack on stuff that tastes like canary mix and we sip on bitter herb tea until we think we're going to gag. By the third day we're so sore we can only trot a half a block . . . so we get up later. The Thanksgiving season brings too many temptations so we fudge . . . and finally gorge. In less than a month, our blimp is back in the hangar. And when the urge to exercise comes over us, we just lie down quietly until the urge goes away.

Sticking with any commitment is costly. And I can assure

you, becoming a servant who gives and gives and gives to others is no exception. By comparison, it will make dieting look like a piece of cake (no pun intended).

Is It Worth It, After All?

Let me encourage you, however, in spite of the high cost of giving and the small number of servant-models you may see around you, to determine to be different. God tells us He "loves a cheerful giver" (2 Cor. 9:7), and He promises us that "he who is generous will be blessed" (Prov. 22:9). Let's believe Him! Deep down inside most Christians I know is a deep-seated desire to release instead of keep . . . to give instead of grab. It is worth *whatever* it takes to let that start happening. Moms, dads, singles, kids, teachers, preachers, businessmen, professionals, blue-collar workers, students—it is worth it! Become a giver . . . and watch God open the hearts of others to Himself. We are never more Godlike than when we give.

Shortly after World War II came to a close, Europe began picking up the pieces. Much of the Old Country had been ravaged by war and was in ruins. Perhaps the saddest sight of all was that of little orphaned children starving in the streets of those war-torn cities.

Early one chilly morning an American soldier was making his way back to the barracks in London. As he turned the corner in his jeep, he spotted a little lad with his nose pressed to the window of a pastry shop. Inside the cook was kneading dough for a fresh batch of doughnuts. The hungry boy stared in silence, watching every move. The soldier pulled his jeep to the curb, stopped, got out, and walked quietly over to where the little fellow was standing. Through the steamed-up window he could see the mouth-watering morsels as they were being pulled from the oven, piping hot. The boy salivated and released a slight groan as he watched the cook place them onto the glass-enclosed counter ever so carefully.

The soldier's heart went out to the nameless orphan as he stood beside him.

"Son . . . would you like some of those?"

The boy was startled.

"Oh, yeah . . . I would!"

The American stepped inside and bought a dozen, put them in a bag, and walked back to where the lad was standing in the foggy cold of the London morning. He smiled, held out the bag, and said simply:

"Here you are."

As he turned to walk away, he felt a tug on his coat. He looked back and heard the child ask quietly:

"Mister . . . *are you God?"*

We are never more like God than when we give.

"God so loved the world, that He gave. . . ."

4

The Servant As a Forgiver

Forgiveness is not an elective in the curriculum of servant-hood. It is a required course, and the exams are always tough to pass.

Several years ago I traveled to Trinity Evangelical Divinity School in search of a pastoral intern. In the process of interviewing a number of men, I met a seminarian I will never forget. As it turned out, I did not select him to come for the summer, but I was extremely impressed with his sensitivity to God. Although young and inexperienced, his spirit was tender and he spoke with gentleness. It was obvious that the Lord was deeply at work in his life. The marks of a servant's heart were clearly visible, so much so I probed to discover why. Among other things he related an incredible, true story that illustrated how God was molding him and shaping him through one of those tough "forgiveness exams." As best as I can remember, here's his story. I'll call him Aaron, not his real name.

Late one spring he was praying about having a significant

ministry the following summer. He asked God for a position to open up on some church staff or Christian organization. Nothing happened. Summer arrived, still nothing. Days turned into weeks, and Aaron finally faced reality—he needed *any* job he could find. He checked the want ads and the only thing that seemed a possibility was driving a bus in southside Chicago . . . nothing to brag about, but it would help with tuition in the fall. After learning the route, he was on his own—a rookie driver in a dangerous section of the city. It wasn't long before Aaron realized just *how* dangerous his job really was.

A small gang of tough kids spotted the young driver, and began to take advantage of him. For several mornings in a row they got on, walked right past him without paying, ignored his warnings, and rode until they decided to get off . . . all the while making smart remarks to him and others on the bus. Finally, he decided that had gone on long enough.

The next morning, after the gang got on as usual, Aaron saw a policeman on the next corner, so he pulled over and reported the offense. The officer told them to pay or get off. They paid . . . but, unfortunately, the policeman got off. And *they* stayed on. When the bus turned another corner or two, the gang assaulted the young driver.

When he came to, blood was all over his shirt, two teeth were missing, both eyes were swollen, his money was gone, and the bus was empty. After returning to the terminal and being given the weekend off, our friend went to his little apartment, sank onto his bed and stared at the ceiling in disbelief. Resentful thoughts swarmed his mind. Confusion, anger, and disillusionment added fuel to the fire of his physical pain. He spent a fitful night wrestling with his Lord.

How can this be? Where's God in all of this? I genuinely want to serve Him. I prayed for a ministry. I was willing to serve Him anywhere, doing anything . . . and *this* is the thanks I get!

On Monday morning Aaron decided to press charges. With the help of the officer who had encountered the gang and several who were willing to testify as witnesses against the thugs, most of them were rounded up and taken to the local county jail. Within a few days there was a hearing before the judge.

In walked Aaron and his attorney plus the angry gang members who glared across the room in his direction. Suddenly he was seized with a whole new series of thoughts. Not bitter ones, but compassionate ones! His heart went out to the guys who had attacked him. Under the Spirit's control he no longer hated them—he pitied them. They needed help, not more hate. What could he do? Or say?

Suddenly, after there had been a plea of guilty, Aaron (to the surprise of his attorney and everybody else in the courtroom) stood to his feet and requested permission to speak.

> Your honor, I would like you to total up all the days of punishment against these men—all the time sentenced against them—and I request that you allow me to go to jail in their place.

The judge didn't know whether to spit or wind his watch. Both attorneys were stunned. As Aaron looked over at the gang members (whose mouths and eyes looked like saucers), he smiled and said quietly, "It's because I forgive you."

The dumbfounded judge, when he reached a level of composure, said rather firmly: "Young man, you're out of order. This sort of thing has never been done before!" To which the young man replied with genius insight:

> Oh, yes, it has, your honor . . . yes, it has. It happened over nineteen centuries ago when a man from Galilee paid the penalty that all mankind deserved.

And then, for the next three or four minutes, without interruption, he explained how Jesus Christ died on our behalf, thereby proving God's love and forgiveness.

He was not granted his request, but the young man visited the gang members in jail, led most of them to faith in Christ, and began a significant ministry to many others in southside Chicago.

He passed a tough exam. And, as a result, a large door of ministry—the very thing he'd prayed for—opened up before him. Through the pain of abuse and assault, Aaron began to get a handle on serving others.

Forgiving (like giving) improves our serve!

GOD'S FORGIVENESS OF US

As we undertake a subject this broad, it's necessary that we limit our thoughts to horizontal forgiveness rather than vertical forgiveness. But instead of ignoring the vertical altogether, perhaps I should briefly explain its significance. Actually, it's God's forgiveness of us that makes possible our forgiving others.

When the penalty of our sin was paid in full by Jesus Christ on the cross, God's wrath was expressed against Him—the One who took our place. God was therefore satisfied in the epochal sacrifice . . . allowing all who would turn, in faith, to the Son of God to be totally, once-for-all, forgiven. Christ's blood washed away our sin. And from the moment we believe on Him, we stand forgiven, relieved of guilt, before a satisfied God, freeing Him to shower upon us His grace and love.

Remember the verse from that grand old song the church has sung for years?

> My sin—oh, the bliss of this glorious tho't—
> My sin—not in part, but the whole,
> Is nailed to the cross and I bear it no more,
> Praise the Lord, praise the Lord, O my soul![1]

That says it well, but not as beautifully as the song from the oldest of all hymnals—The Psalms:

> Bless the Lord, O my soul;
> And all that is within me, bless His holy name.

Bless the Lord, O my soul,
And forget none of His benefits;
   Who pardons all your iniquities;
Who heals all your diseases;
   Who redeems your life from the pit;
Who crowns you with lovingkindness and compassion;
   Who satisfies your years with good things,
So that your youth is renewed like the eagle. . . .
   He has not dealt with us according to our sins,
Nor rewarded us according to our iniquities.
   For high as the heavens are above the earth,
So great is His lovingkindness toward those who fear Him.
   As far as the east is from the west,
So far has He removed our transgressions from us (Ps.
103:1–5, 10–12).

That's what Aaron helped the Chicago gang to understand. They ultimately had little difficulty realizing what Christ accomplished on the cross on their behalf. But what they did not understand at the time was that Aaron could never have done that for them, horizontally, if it had not been for what Christ had already done for Aaron, vertically. Not until we fully accept *and appropriate* God's infinite and complete forgiveness on our behalf can we carry out the things I mention in the rest of this chapter.

OUR FORGIVENESS OF ONE ANOTHER

It isn't long before anyone who gets serious about serving others must come to terms with forgiving others as well. Yes, *must*. As I said earlier, it's a required course in the servanthood curriculum. Since this is such a common occurrence, I find it helpful to break the subject down into manageable parts, with handles I can get hold of.

Only Two Possibilities

When wrong has been done against another person, there are only two possibilities: But whether we are responsible for the offense or are the recipients of it, the first move is always ours. The true servant doesn't keep score. The general principle is set forth in Ephesians 4:31–32, which says:

> Let all bitterness and wrath and anger and clamor and slander be put away from you, along with all malice.
> And be kind to one another, tender-hearted, forgiving each other, just as God in Christ also has forgiven you.

That's a beautiful summation of the whole subject of forgiveness. It describes how to live with a clear conscience and thus be free to serve. And observe the reminder—you forgive others ". . . as God in Christ also has forgiven you" (vertical). But we need to get more specific. Let's analyze both sides of the forgiveness coin.

When You Are the Offender

Matthew 5:23–24 describes, in a nutshell, the correct response and procedure to follow when we have been in the wrong and offended someone.

> If therefore you are presenting your offering at the altar, and there remember that your brother has something against you,
> leave your offering there before the altar, and go your way; first be reconciled to your brother, and then come and present your offering.

The scene is clear. A person in Jesus' day has come to worship. At that time, in keeping with the Jewish law and custom, worshipers brought sacrificial animals or birds with them. The sacrifice would be slain before God, providing cleansing of sin and a way of open access to prayer. Today it would simply be a Christian's coming to his Father in prayer. Either way, the worshiper is suddenly seized with the inescapable thought, the painful realization that he or she has offended another person. In the words of Jesus, you ". . . remember your brother has something against you." What do you do?

Stop! Don't ignore that realization. Don't just plunge on into prayer, even though that may be your first reaction. God wants us, rather, to be sensitive to His quiet prompting.

In verse 24, we are instructed to do four things:

1. Stop   "leave your offering there. . . ."
2. Go   "go your way. . . ."
3. Reconcile   " . . . first be reconciled. . . ."
4. Return   " . . . then come and present your offering. . . ."

The key term is *reconciled.* It's from a Greek root verb that means "to alter, to change" . . . with a prefix attached to the verb that means "through." In other words, we are commanded to go through a process that will result in a change. Clearly, the *offender* is to initiate the action.

One reliable authority defines this word rather vividly: "To change enmity for friendship . . . bringing about mutual concession for mutual hostility."[2] And another, "Seeing to it that the angry brother renounce his enmity. . . ."[3]

That needs little clarification. We are to go (ideally, personally—if not possible, at least by phone or letter) and confess both the wrong and our grief over the offense, seeking the forgiveness of the one we wounded. *Then,* we are free to return to God in worship and prayer.

"But what if he or she won't forgive?" Good question! The important thing for each of us to remember is that you are responsible for *you* and I am responsible for *me.* With the right motive, in the right spirit, at the right time, out of obedience to God, we are to humble ourselves (remember, it is servanthood we're developing) and attempt to make things right. God will honor our efforts. The one offended may need time—first to get over the shock and next, to have God bring about a change in his or her heart. Healing sometimes takes time. Occasionally, a lot of time.

"What if the situation only gets worse?" Another good question frequently asked. This can happen. You see, all the time the one offended has been blaming you . . . mentally sticking pins in your doll . . . thinking all kinds of bad things about you. When you go to make things right, you suddenly cause his internal scales to go out of balance. You take away the blame and all that's left is the person's guilt, which does a number on him, resulting in even worse feelings. But now it's no longer your fault. Illustration? King Saul and young David. In case you don't remember, young David became a threat to the paranoid monarch. No matter how hard he tried to win back the favor of Saul, things only got worse. It took *years* for the troubled king to realize that David was sincere in his efforts to make things right. Again, it may take awhile for God to get through.

"What if I decide to simply deal with it before God and not go through the hassle and embarrassment of talking with the other person?" We'll do *anything* to make things easier, won't we? Well, first off—that is a willful contradiction of the command. Jesus says, "Stop, go, reconcile, and return!" *Not* to go is direct disobedience. It also can result in things getting worse.

Let's say I am driving away from your church parking lot next Sunday morning. I back my car into the side of your beautiful, new *Mercedes 450 SEL.* CRUNCH! You are visiting with friends following the service and you hear the noise. Your stomach churns as you see me get out of the car, look at the damage . . . and then bow in prayer:

> Dear Lord, please forgive me for being so preoccupied and clumsy. And please give John grace as he sees the extensive damage I have caused out of sheer negligence. And provide his needs as he takes this car in to have it fixed. Thanks, Lord. Amen.

As I drive away, I wave and smile real big as I yell out the window, "It's all cleared up, John. I claimed the damage before God. *Isn't grace wonderful!*"

Tell me, how does that grab you? I have rather strong doubts that it would suddenly make things A-O.K., no matter how sincere my prayer might have been. You and I know that would do no good.

When I was a kid in church we used to sing a little chorus

that sounded so pious, so right. In fact, we would often close our youth meetings by holding hands in a circle and sing this piece with our eyes closed:

> If I have wounded any soul today,
> If I have caused one foot to go astray,
> If I have walked in my own willful way
> Dear Lord, forgive![4]

I now question the message of that nice-sounding song. Wounded souls are offended people. And the Savior does not say, "Simply pray and I'll forgive you." In fact, He says, "Stop praying until you have made things right!" That is the part of the "forgiveness exam" that's tough to pass.

One final question before moving on to the other side of the coin: "What if it is impossible for me to reconcile because the offended person has died?" Obviously, you cannot contact the dead. It's impossible to get a hearing, but your conscience still badgers you. In such unique cases, I recommend that you share your burden of guilt with someone whom you can trust. A close friend, your mate, a counselor, or your pastor. Be specific and completely candid. Pray with that individual and confess openly the wrong and the guilt of your soul. In such cases—and only in such cases—prayer and the presence of an understanding, affirming individual will provide the relief you need so desperately.

After David had indirectly murdered Uriah, Bathsheba's husband, his guilt was enormous. Adultery and hypocrisy on top of murder just about did him in. If you want to know the depth of his misery, read Psalm 32:3–4:

> When I kept silent about my sin, my body wasted
>   away
> Through my groaning all day long.
> For day and night Thy hand was heavy upon me;
> My vitality was drained away as with the fever-heat of
>   summer.

Finally, when it all caved in on top of him, when he broke the hypocritical silence and sought God's forgiveness, Uriah was not there to hear his confession. He had been dead the better part of a year. But David was not alone. A prophet named Nathan was there, you may recall. And when the broken king poured out his soul, "I have sinned. . . ," Nathan followed quickly with these affirming words: "The Lord also has taken away your sin; you shall not die" (2 Sam. 12:13).

When you have been the cause of an offense, that is, when you are the offender, have the heart of a servant. Stop, go, reconcile, and then return.

When You Are the Offended

Turn now to Matthew 18:21–35 . . . same book, same teacher, similar subject, but a different style and setting entirely from the Matthew 5 passage where Jesus delivered a monologue communicating a large number of things to His disciples. He touched on each rather generally, all great truths . . . but many subjects. Here in chapter 18 He is engaged in more of a dialogue, dealing in depth with the right response toward someone who offends us. Rather than dump the whole truckload on you, let me present these verses in sections.

First, the disciple's question:

> Then Peter came and said to Him, "Lord, how often shall my brother sin against me and I forgive him? Up to seven times?" (Matt. 18:21).

Good, relevant question. What's the limit we should place on forgiveness? Peter was feeling magnanimous that day, for the going rate (according to the rabbis) was three times.[5] The Jews were instructed to forgive once, forgive twice . . . and a third time, but from then on, forget it. Peter doubled the limit then added a bonus for good measure.

Now, the Lord's response:

. . . I do not say to you, up to seven times, but up to seventy times seven (Matt. 18:22).

Obviously, He is not saying literally, "Would you believe 490, Peter?" No, not that. He's suggesting an *infinite* number of times. *Limitless.* I would imagine that thought blew those disciples away! Which, no doubt, prompted Jesus to go into greater detail. Hence, a parable with a punch line. Read the story very carefully, preferably aloud and slowly.

For this reason the kingdom of heaven may be compared to a certain king who wished to settle accounts with his slaves.

And when he had begun to settle them, there was brought to him one who owed him ten thousand talents.

But since he did not have the means to repay, his lord commanded him to be sold, along with his wife and children and all that he had, and repayment to be made.

The slave therefore falling down, prostrated himself before him, saying, "Have patience with me, and I will repay you everything."

And the lord of that slave felt compassion and released him and forgave him the debt.

But that slave went out and found one of his fellow-slaves who owed him a hundred denarii; and he seized him and began to choke him, saying, "Pay back what you owe."

So his fellow-slave fell down and began to entreat him, saying, "Have patience with me and I will repay you."

He was unwilling however, but went and threw him in prison until he should pay back what was owed.

So when his fellow-slaves saw what had happened, they were deeply grieved and came and reported to their lord all that had happened.

Then summoning him, his lord said to him, "You wicked slave, I forgave you all that debt because you entreated me.

"Should you not also have had mercy on your fellow-slave, even as I had mercy on you?"

And his lord, moved with anger, handed him over to the torturers until he should repay all that was owed him (Matt. 18:23–34).

By now, you have probably begun to think in terms of vertical forgiveness and horizontal forgiveness. The vertical is clearly seen in verses 23 through 27. This was an incredible debt (about $10,000,000!) requiring infinite forgiveness, which the king provided (read verse 27 again)—a beautiful reminder of God's forgiving the sinner.

The horizontal comes in view in verses 28 through 34. That same slave, having just been forgiven that incredible debt, turned against a fellow who owed him *less than twenty bucks* and assaulted the poor fellow. When the king got word of his violent reaction, he was furious. I mean, he was beside himself! And the confrontation that followed was understandably severe.

A couple of things emerge from the latter part of this story that provide us with reasons to forgive others.

1. To refuse to forgive is hypocritical. Note again verses 32 through 33.

> Then summoning him, his lord said to him, "You wicked slave, I forgave you all that debt because you entreated me.
> Should you not also have had mercy on your fellow-slave, even as I had mercy on you?"

Since we have been the recipients of maximum mercy, who are we to suddenly demand justice from others? The compassion God (illustrated in the parable as the king) demonstrates on our behalf calls for us to do the same toward others. Anything less is downright hypocritical.

2. To refuse to forgive inflicts inner torment upon us. Remember how the story ends? It is exceedingly significant. "And his lord, moved with anger, handed him over to the torturers until he should repay all that was owed him."

"Well," you say, "that was just a parable. We can't press every point and say each little detail applies to us." Granted, but in this case, it's not a *little* detail. It's the punch line, the climax of the whole story. How can I say that? Because verse 35 is not part of the parable. It is a statement Jesus makes *after* the story ends. It is His penetrating application of the whole parable on forgiving others.

He wrapped up His instruction with this grim warning: "So shall My heavenly Father also do to you, if each of you does not forgive his brother from your heart."

Frankly, this is one of the most important truths God ever revealed to me on the consequences of an unforgiving spirit. When Jesus says, "So shall My heavenly Father also do to you. . . ," He is referring back to the closing words of the parable, which says:

> And his lord, moved with anger, handed him over to the torturers until he should repay all that was owed him.

This is no fictitious tale, like Bluebeard who tortured others behind a secret door. No, Jesus says God personally will allow those who refuse to forgive others to be tortured.

What in the world does that mean? The root Greek term from which "torturers" is translated is a verb meaning "to torment"— a frightening thought. When I first saw the thing begin to take shape in my mind, I resisted it. I thought, "No, that's too harsh!" But the further I probed, the clearer it became.

The same term is used to describe a person suffering "great pain" (Matt. 8:6). And it is used to describe the misery of a man being "in agony" in hell as he pleads for relief (Luke 16:23–24). When we read of a man named Lot, in 2 Peter 2:8, who was surrounded and oppressed by the conduct of unprincipled men, we read "his righteous soul was tormented day after day. . . ." Again the same term is used. Pain, agony, and torment are all a part of this torturous experience.

But here in Matthew 18:34–35, Jesus refers to tormentors—a noun, not a verb. He is saying the one who refuses to forgive, the Christian who harbors grudges, bitter feelings toward another, will be turned over to torturous thoughts, feelings of misery, and agonizing unrest within. One fine expositor describes it like this:

> This is a marvelously expressive phrase to describe what happens to us when we do not forgive another. It is an accurate description of gnawing resentment and bitterness, the awful gall

of hate or envy. It is a terrible feeling. We cannot get away from it. We feel strongly this separation from another and every time we think of them we feel within the acid of resentment and hate eating away at our peace and calmness. This is the torturing that our Lord says will take place.[6]

And who hasn't endured such feelings? It is one of the horrible consequences of *not* forgiving those who offend us. It makes no difference who it is—one of your parents or in-laws, your pastor or former pastor, a close friend who turned against you, some teacher who was unfair, or a business partner who ripped you off . . . even your former partner in marriage. I meet many divorcees who have been "handed over to the torturers" for this very reason. Believe me, it is not worth the misery. We are to forgive as we have been forgiven! Release the poison of all that bitterness . . . let it gush out before God, and declare the sincere desire to be free. It's one of the major steps each of us must take toward becoming God's model of a servant.

HOW TO MAKE IT HAPPEN

There is enough in this chapter to keep us thinking (and forgiving) for weeks. But there are a couple of specifics that need to be considered before we move ahead.

First, *focus fully on God's forgiveness of you.* Don't hurry through this. Think of how vast, how extensive His mercy has been extended toward you. Like Aaron, the young seminary student, must have done in the courtroom that day. Like David did when he wrote "Hymn 103." He got extremely specific. Remember?

> Bless the Lord, O my soul,
>   And forget none of His benefits;
> Who pardons all your iniquities;
>   Who heals all your diseases;
> Who redeems your life from the pit;
>   Who crowns you with lovingkindness and compassion;
> Who satisfies your years with good things,

So that your youth is renewed like the eagle
He has not dealt with us according to our sins,
Nor rewarded us according to our iniquities.
For high as the heavens are above the earth,
So great is His lovingkindness toward those who
fear Him.
As far as the east is from the west,
So far has He removed our transgressions from us
(Ps. 103:2–5, 10–12).

Meditate on that in your own life. Personalize these words by substituting *me* and *my* for *us* and *your*. Ponder the depth of God's mercy . . . the debts against you He graciously canceled. The extent to which you can envision God's forgiveness of you, to that same measure you will be given the capacity to forgive others.

Next, *deal directly and honestly with any resentment you currently hold against anyone.*

It's a tough exam. But think of the alternative—torturing, agonizing feelings, the churning within, the enormous emotional energy you burn up and waste every day.

Maybe you are willing to go just so far. You will bargain with God and agree to forgive *but not forget.* That is one of the most regrettable mistakes a servant-in-the-making can make. Because limited forgiveness is like conditional love—a poor substitute for the genuine item. It's no forgiveness at all.

Amy Carmichael said it best when she wrote these words:

If I say, "Yes, I forgive, but I cannot forget," as though the God, who twice a day washes all the sands on all the shores of all the world, could not wash such memories from my mind, then I know nothing of Calvary love.[7]

So much for forgiving. We now need to think about forgetting. That's next. If forgiveness is the process God takes us through to heal inner wounds . . . then forgetting would be the removal of the ugly scar.

And God can even do that.

5

The Servant As a Forgetter

I'll forgive . . . but I'll *never* forget." We say and hear that so much that it's easy to shrug it off as "only natural." That's the problem! It is the most natural response we can expect. Not *supernatural.* It also can result in tragic consequences.

Last week I read of two unmarried sisters who lived together, but because of an unresolved disagreement over an insignificant issue, they stopped speaking to each other (one of the inescapable results of refusing to forget). Since they were either unable or unwilling to move out of their small house, they continued to use the same rooms, eat at the same table, use the same appliances, and sleep in the same room . . . all separately . . . without one word. A chalk line divided the sleeping area into two halves, separating doorways as well as the fireplace. Each would come and go, cook and eat, sew and read without ever stepping over into her sister's territory. Through the black of the night, each could hear the deep breathing of the other, but because both were unwilling to take the first step toward forgiving and forgetting the silly offense, they coexisted *for years* in grinding silence.[1]

Refusing to forgive *and forget* leads to other tragedies, like monuments of spite. How many churches split (often over nit-picking issues) then spin off into another direction, fractured, splintered, and blindly opinionated?

After I spoke at a summer Bible conference meeting one evening, a lady told me she and her family had been camping across America. In their travels they drove through a town and passed a church with a name she said she would never forget— THE ORIGINAL CHURCH OF GOD, NUMBER TWO.

Whether a personal or public matter, we quickly reveal whether we possess a servant's heart in how we respond to those who have offended us. And it isn't enough simply to say, "Well, okay—you're forgiven, but don't expect me to forget it!" That means we have erected a monument of spite in our mind, and that isn't really forgiveness at all. Servants must be big people. Big enough to *go on*, remembering the right and forgetting the wrong. Like the age-old saying, "Write injuries in dust, benefits in marble."[2] As we shall see, forgetting also includes other things besides forgetting offenses: doing helpful things for others without expecting something in return . . . being, in the true and noble sense of the term, self-forgetful.

CAN THE MIND EVER FORGET?

A question flashes through my head as I write these words: Can our minds actually *allow* us to forget? The way God has made us—with that internal filing system we call "memory"—it is doubtful we can fully forget even the things we *want* to forget.

Our minds are simply remarkable. Dr. Earl Radmacher aptly illustrates the truth of that statement:

> The human mind is a fabulous computer. As a matter of fact, no one has been able to design a computer as intricate and efficient as the human mind. Consider this: your brain is capable

of recording 800 memories per second for seventy-five years without ever getting tired. . . .

I have heard some persons complain that their brain is too tired to get involved in a program of Scripture memorization. I have news for them—the body can get tired, but the brain never does. A human being doesn't use more than 2 percent of his brain power, scientists tell us. And, of course, some demonstrate this fact more obviously than others. The point is, the brain is capable of an incredible amount of work and it retains everything it takes in. You never really forget anything; you just don't recall it. Everything is on permanent file in your brain.[3]

Because of facts like those, we need to understand that I'm not referring to forgetting in the technical or literal sense of the term. Rather, I'm thinking about forgetting the same way Paul does in 1 Corinthians 13:4–5 when he says:

Love is patient, love is kind, and is not jealous; love does not brag and is not arrogant, does not act unbecomingly; it does not seek its own, is not provoked, does not take into account a wrong suffered.

That last statement is rendered this way in the J. B. Phillips translation:

This love of which I speak is slow to lose patience—it looks for a way of being constructive. It is not possessive: it is neither anxious to impress nor does it cherish inflated ideas of its own importance.

Love has good manners and does not pursue selfish advantage. It is not touchy. It does not keep account of evil or gloat over the wickedness of other people. On the contrary, it is glad with all good men when truth prevails.

True servants, when demonstrating genuine love, don't keep score. Webster defines *forget* as "to lose the remembrance of . . . to treat with inattention or disregard . . . to disregard intentionally: OVERLOOK: to cease remembering or noticing . . . to fail to become mindful at the proper time."[4] That's the thought.

A couple of scriptures illustrate and encourage this great-hearted virtue.

> Those who love Thy law have great peace,
> And nothing causes them to stumble (Ps. 119:165).

The psalmist openly declares that those who possess a deep love for God's Word will have great measures of His *shalom* . . . and, in addition, they will be big enough to resist stumbling over offenses.

Jesus hinted at this when He spoke out against a judgmental spirit. Read His words carefully.

> Do not judge lest you be judged yourselves.
> For in the way you judge, you will be judged; and by your standard of measure, it shall be measured to you.
> And why do you look at the speck in your brother's eye, but do not notice the log that is in your own eye?
> Or how can you say to your brother, "Let me take the speck out of your eye," and behold, the log is in your own eye?
> You hypocrite, first take the log out of your own eye; and then you will see clearly enough to take the speck out of your brother's eye (Matt. 7:1–5).

So then, as we talk about "forgetting" let's understand that we mean:

- Refusing to keep score (1 Cor. 13:5).
- Being bigger than any offense (Ps. 119:165).
- Harboring no judgmental attitude (Matt. 7:1–5).

Before proceeding, a positive thought is in order. We also have in mind the ability to go on beyond our own good deeds. Once they are done, they're done. No need to drop little hints on how thoughtful we were. Improving our serve includes forgetting our service.

A Close Look at Forgetting

Tucked away in the New Testament is a chapter that illustrates this truth beautifully. It's Philippians, chapter 3. The writer, Paul, is listing a number of things in his past that could be food for pride.

> . . . If anyone else has a mind to put confidence in the flesh, I far more: circumcised the eighth day, of the nation of Israel, of the tribe of Benjamin, a Hebrew of Hebrews; as to the Law, a Pharisee; as to zeal, a persecutor of the church, as to the righteousness which is in the Law, found blameless (vv. 4–6).

If you were looking for somebody to give a testimony next Sunday, Paul would be a winner. In fact, if he were not careful, he could turn it into a "braggimony." These are impressive facts . . . and they are absolutely true.

But Paul, servant that he was, kept it all in proper perspective.

> But whatever things were gain to me, those things I have counted as loss for the sake of Christ.
> More than that, I count all things to be loss in view of the surpassing value of knowing Christ Jesus my Lord, for whom I have suffered the loss of all things, and count them but rubbish in order that I may gain Christ (vv. 7–9).

In comparison to Jesus Christ and all the things He has made possible—His forgiveness, His love, His righteousness—everything else *we* may be or accomplish diminishes in significance. Paul's following words describe the healthy humility of a servant:

> I don't mean to say I am perfect. I haven't learned all I should even yet, but I keep working toward that day when I will finally be all that Christ saved me for and wants me to be.
> No, dear brothers, I am still not all I should be but I am bringing all my energies to bear on this one thing: Forgetting the

past and looking forward to what lies ahead, I strain to reach the end of the race and receive the prize for which God is calling us up to heaven because of what Christ Jesus did for us (vv. 12–14, TLB).

Woven into those words are these three statements:
1. "I have not arrived."
2. "I forget what is behind."
3. "I move on to what is ahead."
Within each of these three statements, I find an important characteristic of servanthood: vulnerability, humility, and determination.

Vulnerability

"I have not arrived" is a concept that Paul mentions no less than three times in Philippians 3:12–13:
1. *"Not that I have already obtained it . . ."* (v. 12).
2. *". . . or have already become perfect . . ."* (v. 12).
3. *". . . I do not regard myself as having laid hold of it . . ."* (v. 13).

How refreshing!

Here is this brilliant, competent, gifted, strong leader who freely declares, "I don't have everything wired." Vulnerability includes more than this, however. It means being willing to express personal needs, admitting one's own limitations or failures, having a teachable spirit, and *especially* being reluctant to appear the expert, the answer man, the final voice of authority. Not only are these traits refreshing, they're rare!

If you're the type that always has to come out right . . . if you have the need to be "perfect," then you will always be in the position of having something to prove. And others around you must do the same.

Executive Howard Butt, a businessman in Corpus Christi, Texas, writes of this in a very honest and practical manner:

If your leadership is Christian you can openly reveal your failures. Leaders who are fully human do not hide their sins.

Within you operates the principle of the cross, the modus operandi of strength in weakness.

This principle points up our problem—we who are religious. We want a Christian reputation more than we want Christ. And yet our Lord, becoming sin for us, "made himself of no reputation." . . .

Am I willing to hide my strengths and reveal my weaknesses? Are you? Telling our triumphs, our successes, our achievements, we glorify ourselves. . . .

Bragging about my goodness, I build barriers up; when I confess my sins, those barriers come down. Pagan outsiders get driven away by our pious parade of religious achievements. Building our high walls of intimidation, we make their friendly corner bartender look good. Christians are not half-angels with high-beam halos, but real live forgiven sinners up close. . . .

Christ's death frees you from hiding your sins. You can be vulnerable and open. When you are weak then you are strong. You shake the darkness with irresistible blows: the divine might of weakness. You hit your hardest when your guard is down.[5]

Being vulnerable is part of being a servant who forgets.

Humility

"I forget what is behind" is a statement that assures us Paul was not the type to live in the past. He says, in effect, "I disregard my own accomplishments as well as others' offenses against me. I refuse to dwell on that." This requires humility. Especially so when you examine Paul's past. Just listen:

Five times I received from the Jews thirty-nine lashes.

Three times I was beaten with rods, once I was stoned, three times I was shipwrecked, a night and a day I have spent in the deep.

I have been on frequent journeys, in dangers from rivers, dangers from robbers, dangers from my countrymen, dangers from the Gentiles, dangers in the city, dangers in the wilderness, dangers on the sea, dangers among false brethren; I have been in labor and hardship, through many sleepless nights, in hunger and thirst, often without food, in cold and exposure (2 Cor. 11:24–27).

Think of all the people Paul could have included on his "hate list." But he had no such list. With humility, he forgot what was behind him. He intentionally disregarded all those wrongs against him.

The very best example I can think of is a remarkable man named Joseph in the book of Genesis. Rejected and hated by his brothers, sold to a group of travelers in a caravan destined for Egypt, sold again as a common slave in the Egyptian market, falsely accused by Potiphar's wife, forgotten in a dungeon, and considered dead by his own father, this man was finally promoted to a position of high authority just beneath the Pharaoh. *If anybody ever had a reason to nurse his wounds and despise his past, Joseph was the man!*

But the amazing part of the story is this: He refused to remember the offenses. In fact, when he and his wife had their first child, he named the boy *Manasseh,* a Hebrew name that meant "forget." He explains the reason he chose the name:

> And Joseph named the first-born Manasseh, "For," he said, "God has made me forget all my trouble and all my father's household" (Gen. 41:51).

His words include an extremely important point. In order for us to forget wrongs done against us, God must do the erasing.

Isaiah, the prophet of Judah, puts it in these terms:

> Fear not, for you will not be put to shame;
> Neither feel humiliated, for you will not be disgraced;
> But you will forget the shame of your youth,
> And the approach of your widowhood you will
> remember no more.
> For your husband is your Maker,
> Whose name is the Lord of hosts;
> And your redeemer is the Holy One of Israel,
> Who is called the God of all the earth (Isa. 54:4–5).

The Lord God promises us we can forget because He personally will take the place of those painful memories. To you who have had a shameful youth, to you who have lost your mate, the living Lord will replace those awful memories *with Himself.* Great promise! That makes the forgetting possible. Left to ourselves, no way! But with the promise that God will replace the pain with Himself—His presence, His power, His very life—we can "forget what lies behind."

There is yet another characteristic of good servants in addition to vulnerability and humility. It's implied in the words "I press on toward the goal . . ." (Phil. 3:14).

Determination

Those servants who refuse to get bogged down in and anchored to the past are those who pursue the objectives of the future. People who do this are seldom petty. They are too involved in getting a job done to be occupied with yesterday's hurts and concerns. Very near the end of his full and productive life, Paul wrote: "I have fought the good fight, I have finished the course, I have kept the faith" (2 Tim. 4:7). What a grand epitaph! He seized every day by the throat. He relentlessly pursued life.

I know human nature well enough to realize that some people excuse their bitterness over past hurts by thinking, "It's too late to change. I've been injured and the wrong done against me is too great for me ever to forget it. Maybe Paul could press on— not me!" A person with this mind-set is convinced that he or she is the exception to the truths of this chapter and is determined not to change because "life has dealt him or her a bad hand."

But when God holds out hope, when God makes promises, when God says, "It can be done," there are *no exceptions.* With each new dawn there is delivered to your door a fresh, new package called "today." God has designed us in such a way that we can handle only one package at a time . . . and all the grace we need will be supplied by Him as we live out that day.

I cannot recall reading a more moving illustration of this truth than the true story John Edmund Haggai tells regarding the tragic birth and life of his son. I share it with you in detail with the hope that at least one person will discover the all-important secret of pressing on one day at a time.

The Lord graciously blessed us with a precious son. He was paralyzed and able to sit in his wheelchair only with the assistance of full-length body braces. One of the nation's most respected gynecologists and obstetricians brought him into the world. Tragically, this man—overcome by grief—sought to find the answer in a bourbon bottle rather than in a blessed Bible. Due to the doctor's intoxication at the time of delivery, he inexcusably bungled his responsibility. Several of the baby's bones were broken. His leg was pulled out at the growing center. Needless abuse—resulting in hemorrhaging of the brain—was inflicted upon the little fellow. (Let me pause long enough to say that this is no indictment upon doctors. I thank God for doctors. This man was a tragic exception. He was banned from practice in some hospitals, and, as mentioned previously, he committed suicide.)

During the first year of the little lad's life, eight doctors said he could not possibly survive. For the first two years of his life my wife had to feed him every three hours with a Brecht feeder. It took a half hour to prepare for the feeding and it took another half hour to clean up and put him back to bed. Not once during that time did she ever get out of the house for any diversion whatsoever. Never did she get more than two hours sleep at one time.

My wife, formerly Christine Barker of Bristol, Virginia, had once been acclaimed by some of the nation's leading musicians as one of the outstanding contemporary female vocalists in America. From the time she was thirteen she had been popular as a singer— and constantly in the public eye. Hers was the experience of receiving and rejecting some fancy offers with even fancier incomes to marry an aspiring Baptist pastor with no church to pastor!

Then, after five years of marriage, tragedy struck! The whole episode was so unnecessary. Eight of the nation's leading doctors said that our son could not survive. From a life of public service she was now marooned within the walls of our home. Her beautiful voice no longer enraptured public audiences with the story of Jesus, but was now silenced, or at best, muted to the subdued humming of lullabies.

Had it not been from her spiritual maturity whereby she laid hold of the resources of God and lived one day at a time, this heart-rending experience would long since have caused an emotional breakdown.

John Edmund, Jr., our little son, lived more than twenty years. We rejoice that he committed his heart and life to Jesus Christ and gave evidence of a genuine concern for the things of the Lord. I attribute his commitment to Jesus Christ and his wonderful disposition to the sparkling radiance of an emotionally mature, Christ-centered mother who has mastered the discipline of living one day at a time. Never have I—nor has anyone else— heard a word of complaint from her. The people who know her concur that at thirty-five years of age and after having been subjected to more grief than many people twice her age, she possessed sparkle that would be the envy of any high school senior and the radiance and charm for which any debutante would gladly give a fortune.

Seize today. Live for today. Wring it dry of every opportunity.[6]

A CHALLENGE: TWO QUESTIONS

In these last three chapters we have considered the servant in three separate yet related roles: as a giver, as a forgiver, and as a forgetter. Of the three, I honestly believe the third is the most exacting. The other two bring with them benefits and blessings that encourage us almost immediately. But forgetting is some- thing shared with no other person. It's a solo flight. And all the rewards are postponed until eternity . . . but how great they will be on that day! Forgetting requires the servant to think correctly—something we'll deal with in the next chapter— which means our full focus must be on the Lord and not on humanity. By God's great grace, it can happen.

Before reading on, let's pause long enough to ask ourselves two questions:

1. Is there someone or something I have refused to forget, which keeps me from being happy and productive?

If your answer is yes, stop and declare it openly to your Lord, asking Him to take away the pain and the bitterness.

2. Am I a victim of self-pity, living out my days emotionally paralyzed in anguish and despair?

If your answer is yes, stop and consider the consequences of living the rest of your life excusing your depression rather than turning it all over to the only One who can remove it.

And lest you are still convinced it's "too late" . . . you are "too old to change" . . . your situation is "too much to overcome," just listen to these immortal lines from Longfellow:

> "It is too late!" Ah, nothing is too late—
> Cato learned Greek at eighty; Sophocles
> Wrote his grand "Oedipus," and Simonides
> Bore off the prize of verse from his compeers
> When each had numbered more than fourscore years;
> And Theophrastus, at fourscore and ten,
> Had begun his "Characters of Men."
> Chaucer, at Woodstock, with his nightingales,
> At sixty wrote the "Canterbury Tales".
> Goethe, at Weimar, toiling to the last,
> Completed "Faust" when eighty years were past.
> What then? Shall we sit idly down and say,
> "The night has come; it is no longer day"?
> For age is opportunity no less
> Than youth itself, though in another dress.
> And as the evening twilight fades away,
> The sky is filled with stars, invisible by day.

It is never too late to start doing what is right. Never.

6

Thinking Like
a Servant Thinks

About now, some of you may be getting a little nervous.

All this talk about serving and giving and releasing rights and putting down self sounds okay for awhile. It's part of the whole Christian package. It's expected, to an extent. But isn't it possible to go overboard on stuff like this? Aren't there some people who will take advantage of servants and turn them into slaves? You bet there are!

Not Mind-Control Slavery

In fact, that is the ace trump among cultic leaders. The secret of their success is mind control. They want your mind, and they are not satisfied until they have absolute control over it. The ultimate control is behavior modification, which is just another word for brainwashing. A perfect example? The People's Temple under the twisted leadership of the late Jim Jones. May God help us *never* to forget that whole tragic episode!

Jack Sparks calls these cultic leaders "mindbenders," an appropriate title. In his book he describes the common method of mind control as a three-step program—not three steps in sequence, but three steps that occur simultaneously.

Step 1 is "deprogramming" . . . convincing you that your past is all wrong. What you always thought was right is wrong, wrong, wrong!

Step 2 calls for the complete subjugation of the will. This takes time. During the process a cult member learns the technique of putting the mind into neutral, sort of a "freewheeling" experience—perfect preparation for the third step.

Step 3 is the "reprogramming" phase. It is concentrated, intensive teaching (*indoctrination* is a better word) designed to replace old concepts with new ones.[1]

The result, of course, is a far cry from the role of a servant we've been considering. That form of cultic mindbending turns a human being into a puppet, a slave without personal dignity, without the privilege to think and to ask questions, and without the joy of serving others willingly under the control and authority of Jesus Christ. The thought of being enslaved to a guru and his or her demanding system of thought is something that ought to strike fear into all of us. If you question that, I suggest you read the incredible story of Christopher Edwards as he became a helpless pawn in the hands of one of the most insidious cults on the rise today. Not until the man was kidnapped was there any hope of recovery.

This bright, clear-thinking Yale graduate became virtually a glob of human putty in the hands of the "Moonies" in Northern California. Without realizing what was happening to him, the cultic system took him through the three-step process I just described. After his father and a group of trained professionals finally snatched him from the tight fist of that cult, it took a full year of intense therapy before Chris regained his equilibrium. He tells it all in his book *Crazy for God.*[2]

No, blind loyalty is not servanthood. Believe me, not only am I strongly opposed to the "mind bending" employed by cultic leaders, I see dangers in other ministries that take unfair advantage of people—ministries we'd certainly not think of as cults. Any ministry that requires blind loyalty and unquestioning obedience is suspect. Not all gurus are in the eastern religions, you know. Some discipleship ministries, quite frankly, come dangerously near this point. Now I am not discrediting all discipleship programs! To do so would be unfair. As a matter of fact, I personally benefited from an outstanding discipling ministry many years ago. Furthermore, we encourage a broad discipleship program in our own church here in Fullerton, California. My main concern is the abuse of power, over-emphasis of loyalty to a human leader, an intense and unhealthy accountability that uses intimidation, fear, and guilt to promote authoritarianism. Weak and meek people can become the prey of such paranoid, self-appointed messiahs, resulting not in spiritual growth, but in exploitation and the loss of human dignity.

Ronald M. Enroth describes it rather well:

> For people who have lacked positive structure in their lives, who have difficulty making decisions or resolving conflicts or who are just plain uncertain about the future, these movements/churches/programs are a haven.
>
> The leaders of many of these groups consciously foster an unhealthy form of dependency, spiritually and otherwise, by focusing on themes of submission and obedience to those in authority. They create the impression that people just aren't going to find their way through life's maze without a lot of firm directives from those at the top.[3]

People in the pew and pastors alike need to beware of "bionic" leaders with an abundance of charisma. We need to watch out for the highly gifted, capable, winsome, and popular superstars who focus attention on themselves or their organization. Rather, the true leader must consciously turn people's devotion and worship to the Head of the body—Jesus Christ. The Savior is the Lord. He shares that preeminent place of authority and glory with none other.

And He is before all things, and in Him all things hold together.

He is also head of the body, the church; and He is the beginning, the first-born from the dead; so that He Himself might come to have first place in everything. . . .

And we proclaim Him, admonishing every man and teaching every man with all wisdom, that we may present every man complete in Christ (Col. 1:17–18, 28).

A "Renewed Mind" Is Essential

With that cleared up we are now ready for some positive input on the correct mentality of a servant. Is it possible to think so much like Christ that our minds operate on a different plane than others around us? Not only is it possible—it's essential!

The familiar words of Paul in Romans 12:1–2 need to be reviewed.

I urge you therefore, brethren, by the mercies of God, to present your bodies a living and holy sacrifice, acceptable to God, which is your spiritual service of worship.

And do not be conformed to this world, but be transformed by the renewing of your mind, that you may prove what the will of God is, that which is good and acceptable and perfect.

At this point in his letter to the believers in Rome, Paul drops to his knees, as it were, and *pleads.* That means it's important, perhaps one of the most important truths he would ever write. After urging us to present ourselves to God as living sacrifices, he adds a warning:

Don't let the world around you squeeze you into its own mold, but let God remold your minds from within, so that you may prove in practice that the plan of God for you is good, meets all his demands and moves toward the goal of true maturity (Rom. 12:2, Phillips).

Stop being squeezed in! Quit aping the system of thought that surrounds you, its line of reasoning, its method of operation, its style and techniques! How? By a radical transformation within. By a renewed thought pattern that demonstrates authentic godlikeness. Living differently begins with thinking differently. A life that is characterized by serving others begins in a mind that is convinced of such a life. That explains why that great section of Scripture describing Christ's willingness to take upon Himself the form of a servant begins with the words: "Let this mind be in you, which was also in Christ Jesus . . ." (Phil. 2:5, KJV).

Jesus' life of serving was the outworking of His mind— "unsqueezed" by the world system in all its selfishness—and remains, forever, our example to follow.

For *us* to be true servants, our minds must be renewed.

NATURAL THINKING IN TODAY'S WORLD

Instead of flashing from one scripture to another, let's settle in on a single passage and digest it carefully. One of the most helpful on the subject of the mind is 2 Corinthians 10:1–7. Take a few moments to read and meditate on these seven verses.

Now I, Paul myself urge you by the meekness and gentleness of Christ,—I who am meek when face to face with you, but bold toward you when absent!—

I ask that when I am present I may not be bold with the confidence with which I propose to be courageous against some, who regard us as if we walked according to the flesh.

For though we walk in the flesh, we do not war according to the flesh, for the weapons of our warfare are not of the flesh, but divinely powerful for the destruction of fortresses.

We are destroying speculations and every lofty thing raised up against the knowledge of God, and we are taking every thought captive to the obedience of Christ, and we are ready to punish all disobedience, whenever your obedience is complete.

You are looking at things as they are outwardly. If any one is confident in himself that he is Christ's, let him consider this again within himself, that just as he is Christ's, so also are we.

The Corinthian Christians were an ornery lot! Although born again, they often operated in the realm of carnality because they had a secular mentality. To borrow from Romans 12, they were "in the mold" of the world system . . . their minds were "unrenewed." At times you would have sworn they weren't even in the family of God. For example, they fought with one another, they criticized Paul, they were competitive in the church, and they winked at gross immorality in their midst.

In this section of Paul's letter to them, he points out several of the ways they revealed natural thinking. I find five characteristics:

1. They were prejudiced instead of objective (v. 2).
2. They focused on the visible rather than the invisible (v. 3).
3. They relied on human strength, not divine power (v. 4).
4. They listened to men instead of God (v. 5).
5. They perceived things superficially rather than deeply (v. 7).

When our carnality is in gear, Paul's comments aptly describe our mind-set: surface judgment, shallow thinking, lack of depth, closed, independent, overly impressed with humanity, spiritually out of focus. When we get "squeezed into the mold," the world does a number on us, doesn't it?

Mental Barriers to God's Voice

Actually, God's message gets muffled. Our minds pick up on the strong secular signals so easily that we subconsciously tune Him out. It comes naturally. The passage in 2 Corinthians 10 sets forth a vivid description of the mental barriers that block out His directives and His counsel.

Look closely. Four terms are used by Paul which we need to

understand. If you have a pencil handy, circle each in your Bible: *fortress . . . speculations . . . lofty thing . . . thought.*

A little historical background is needed. In ancient days a city, in order to prosper, needed a security system to protect it from enemy attack. Of primary importance was a wall which restrained enemy troops from invading and which also served as a major means of defense in battle. Guards needed to be on constant watch from their sentinel posts on the wall. There needed to be towers within the city high enough for those inside to see over the wall. And finally at the time of attack, men of military savvy and battle knowledge were needed to give orders and to direct the troops in the heat of combat from within the protection of those towers.

Paul drew a series of analogies from that familiar scene of his day . . . but remember, he's not dealing with a city, but rather with our minds.

Analogy No. 1: The Wall, Our Mental "Fortress"

As the Spirit of God attempts to communicate His truth to us (biblical information on servanthood, for example), He runs up against our "wall," our overall mental attitude, our natural mind-set. For some it's prejudice. With others, it's limited thinking or a negative mentality. Whatever, it is a huge mental barrier that resists divine input just as firmly as a massive stone wall once resisted the invading troops. We all have our *fortresses.* And occasionally we get downright obnoxious as we operate under the control of our "walled fortress."

A tramp discovered that one day when he was looking for a handout in a picturesque old English village. Hungry almost to the point of fainting, he stopped by a pub bearing the classic name, *Inn of St. George and the Dragon.*

"Please, ma'am, could you spare me a bite to eat?" he asked the lady who answered his knock at the kitchen door.

"A bite to eat?" she growled. "For a sorry, no-good bum—a foul-smelling beggar? No!" she snapped as she almost slammed the door on his hand.

Halfway down the lane the tramp stopped, turned around, and eyed the words, St. George and the Dragon. He went back and knocked again on the kitchen door.

"Now what do you want?" the woman asked angrily.

"Well, ma'am, if St. George is in, may I speak with him this time?"

Ouch.

Analogy No. 2: The Guards, Our Mental "Speculations"

Along with the wall-like fortresses, we have natural, human-istic reasonings that give the wall additional strength—defense mechanisms, rationalization, and other thinking patterns that are habitual to us. In Romans 2:15 we read of two such "guards"—blaming and justifying. One reliable authority states that the Greek term translated speculation suggests "the con-templation of actions as a result of the verdict of conscience."[4]

As the Lord God pushes His truth to enter (and thus "renew") our minds, our habitual reflex "guards" the entrance of such alien thoughts! This explains why there is often such a battle that rages when biblical truth is introduced into a mind that has been walled and guarded by years of secularized thinking. We defend the old rather than consider and accept the new.

This could have happened in your own mind when you read chapter 4 on forgiveness. You read what the Bible teaches us to do when we have offended someone. More than likely, you found yourself resisting and defending. I certainly did when I first discovered those truths! We would much rather blame the other person than accept our responsibility. Our "speculations" work like that. They put up a guard against change, causing us to rationalize and justify our actions.

Analogy No. 3: The Towers, Our Mental "Lofty Things"

Accompanying the resistance of our internal wall and guards are "lofty things" that reinforce our defense system from within.

It's the idea of a thing lifted up or exalted. What comes to your mind right now? How about *pride?* And those things pride prompts: argumentation, an unteachable spirit, stubbornness, and refusal to change. As the principles of the Scripture are declared, our natural, unrenewed minds not only resist them, they ask, "Who needs that?" or "I've gotten along pretty good up 'til now." Lofty things—things that are "raised up against the knowledge of God," as Paul put it (2 Cor. 10:5).

Analogy No. 4: The Strategic Men, Our Mental "Thoughts"

Along with the mental wall of habitual resistance, the humanistic reasonings that give it strength, and the proud, lofty reactions that keep the truths of Scripture at arm's length, there are actual thoughts, techniques, devices we employ that push away His Word and His promptings. For example, we have formed the habit of getting even rather than overlooking wrong done against us. So when we come across scriptural instruction that suggests an alternate plan, our inner reaction is "No way!" When God's counsel encourages us to be generous, to release rather than keep, we can think of half a dozen reasons it won't work. It's like having a "Murphy's Law" mentality that is immediately ready to spring into action. This keeps us from deciding favorably toward God.

A vital point I don't want you to miss is that we really have no reason whatsoever to keep serving our secular mentality. We have been freed. Gloriously freed! Before salvation we had no hope. We were victims of all those impulses and defenses within us. But at the cross, our Savior and Lord defeated the enemy. He said, "It is finished," *and it was!* No longer does sin reign as victor. But, you see, our old nature doesn't want us to believe that. It resists *all* messages that would give us freedom. "All *renewed mind* information is to be muffled," commands the old man within us. And with every effort, he puts up a wall, guards, towers, and thoughts to turn all such input away.

And do you realize what our old nature resists the most? It is revealed in verse 5 of 2 Corinthians 10: ". . . taking every thought captive to the obedience of Christ." When that happens, the "renewed mind" is in full operation . . . and it is marvelous! At that moment servanthood is neither irksome nor a thing to be feared. It flows freely.

Listen to a story—fictitious though it is—that Larry Christenson tells. It will help you understand the victory a "renewed mind" provides:

Think of yourself as living in an apartment house. You live there under a landlord who has made your life miserable. He charges you exorbitant rent. When you can't pay, he loans you money at a fearful rate of interest, to get you even further into his debt. He barges into your apartment at all hours of the day and night, wrecks and dirties the place up, then charges you extra for not maintaining the premises. Your life is miserable.

Then comes Someone who says, "I've taken over this apartment house. I've purchased it. You can live here as long as you like, free. The rent is paid up. I am going to be living here with you, in the manager's apartment."

What a joy! You are saved! You are delivered out of the clutches of the old landlord!

But what happens? You hardly have time to rejoice in your new-found freedom, when a knock comes at the door. And there he is—the old landlord! Mean, glowering, and demanding as ever. He has come for the rent, he says.

What do you do? Do you pay him? Of course, you don't! Do you go out and pop him on the nose? No—he's bigger than you are!

You confidently tell him, "You'll have to take that up with the new Landlord." He may bellow, threaten, wheedle, and cajole. You just quietly tell him, "Take it up with the new Landlord." If he comes back a dozen times, with all sorts of threats and arguments, waving legal-looking documents in your face, you simply tell him yet once again, "Take it up with the new Landlord." In the end he has to. He knows it, too. He just hopes that he can bluff and threaten and deceive you into doubting that the new Landlord will really take care of things.

Now this is the situation of a Christian. Once Christ has delivered you from the power of sin and the devil, you can depend on it: that old landlord will soon come back knocking at your door. And what is your defense? How do you keep him from getting the whip hand over you again? You send him to the new Landlord. *You send him to Jesus.*[5]

When Jesus Christ truly takes charge of our minds, bringing our every thought captive to Him, we become spiritually invincible. We operate with supernatural power. We walk under God's complete control.

SUPERNATURAL ABILITY OF THE "RENEWED MIND"

As God's truth penetrates, displacing those mental barriers, we receive several very exciting benefits. In fact, I find two of them named by Paul right here in the 2 Corinthians 10 passage—divine power (v. 4) and authentic independence (vv. 11–12).

We get the distinct impression while reading these verses that nothing on this earth can intimidate us. The New International Version helps clarify this supernatural ability of the "renewed mind":

> For though we live in the world, we do not wage war as the world does. The weapons we fight with are not the weapons of the world. On the contrary, they have divine power to demolish strongholds. We demolish arguments and every pretension that sets itself up against the knowledge of God, and we take captive every thought to make it obedient to Christ (2 Cor. 10:3–5).

Divine Power

Did you catch the reality of divine power in verse 4? Servants with renewed minds have a perspective on life and a power to live life that is altogether unique—divinely empowered.

That explains how wrongs can be forgiven, and how offenses can be forgotten, and how objectives can be pursued day in and day out without our quitting. It's divine power. God promises that He will pour His power into us (Phil. 4:13) and supply all we need if we will simply operate under His full control. When we think correctly we instantly begin to respond correctly.

How can we "demolish" those things that once blew us away? With Christ living out His very life through ours, that's how. By His power we can give ourselves away again and again and again. And we won't fear the outcome. We won't even feel slighted when we don't get the same treatment in return. Servants, remember, don't "keep score." Dale Galloway tells a story in *Dream a New Dream* that beautifully illustrates this point.

Little Chad was a shy, quiet young fella. One day he came home and told his mother, he'd like to make a valentine for everyone in his class. Her heart sank. She thought, "I wish he wouldn't do that!" because she had watched the children when they walked home from school. Her Chad was always behind them. They laughed and hung on to each other and talked to each other. But Chad was never included. Nevertheless, she decided she would go along with her son. So she purchased the paper and glue and crayons. For three whole weeks, night after night, Chad painstakingly made thirty-five valentines.

Valentine's Day dawned, and Chad was beside himself with excitement! He carefully stacked them up, put them in a bag, and bolted out the door. His mom decided to bake him his favorite cookies and serve them up warm and nice with a cool glass of milk when he came home from school. She just knew he would be disappointed . . . maybe that would ease the pain a little. It hurt her to think that he wouldn't get many valentines—maybe none at all.

That afternoon she had the cookies and milk on the table. When she heard the children outside she looked out the window. Sure enough here they came, laughing and having the best time. And, as always, there was Chad in the rear. He walked a little faster than usual. She fully expected him to burst into tears as soon as he got inside. His arms were empty, she noticed, and when the door opened she choked back the tears.

"Mommy has some warm cookies and milk for you."

But he hardly heard her words. He just marched right on by, his face aglow, and all he could say was:

"Not a one . . . not a one."

Her heart sank.

And then he added, "I didn't forget a one, not a single one!"[6]

So it is when God is in control of the servant's mind. We realize as never before that life's greatest joy is to give His love away—a thought that brings to mind the saying:

> It isn't a song until it's sung.
> It isn't a bell until it's rung,
> It isn't love until it's given away!

Authentic Independence

Look at verses 11 and 12 in 2 Corinthians 10:

Let such a person consider this, that what we are in word by letters when absent, such persons we are also in deed when present.

For we are not bold to class or compare ourselves with some of those who commend themselves; but when they measure themselves by themselves, and compare themselves with themselves, they are without understanding.

Isn't that refreshing? No masks of hypocrisy. Not in competition with other believers—not even caught in the trap of comparing himself with others. It all comes to those with a "renewed mind" . . . those who determine they are going to allow the Spirit of God to invade all those walls and towers, capturing the guards that have kept Him at arm's length all these years.

I can't recall the precise date when these truths began to fall into place, but I distinctly remember how I began to change deep within. My fierce tendency to compete with others started to diminish. My insecure need to win—*always* win—also started to fade. Less and less was I interested in comparing myself with other speakers and pastors. This growing, healthy independence freed me to be *me*, not a mixture of what I thought others expected me to be. And now my heart really goes out to others when I see in them that misery-making "comparison syndrome" that held me in its grip for so many years. Not until I started thinking biblically did this independent identity begin to take shape.

SERVANTHOOD STARTS IN THE MIND

Wouldn't you love to live courageously in spite of the odds? Doesn't it sound exciting to be divinely powerful in day-to-day living? Aren't you anxious to become independently authentic in a day of copy-cat styles and horrendous peer pressure? Of course!

It all begins in *the mind*. Let me repeat it one more time: Thinking right always precedes acting right. That is why I have emphasized throughout this chapter the importance of the renewed mind. It is really impossible to grasp the concept of serving others—or to carry it out with joy, without fear—until our minds are freed from the world's mold and transformed by the Lord's power.

I began this chapter with a warning against falling under the spell of a mind-controlling guru. Hopefully, there is no misunderstanding with where I stand on that twisted concept of exploiting others yet calling it servanthood. I feel the need, however, to end with another warning. Not against becoming a victim of some strong personality . . . but against anyone who might "use" others to accomplish his purposes. How easy it is to encourage servanthood so others might serve us. That is not the way our Master walked and neither should we.

I admire the honesty of the man who wrote these words:

> I am like James and John.
> Lord, I size up other people
>   in terms of what they can do for me;

how they can further my program,
 feed my ego,
 satisfy my needs,
 give me strategic advantage.

I exploit people,
 ostensibly for your sake,
 but really for my own sake.

Lord, I turn to you
 to get the inside track
 and obtain special favors,
  your direction for my schemes,
  your power for my projects,
  your sanction for my ambitions,
  your blank check for whatever I want.
I am like James and John.

 Change me, Lord.
 Make me a man who asks of you and of
  others,
  what can I do for you?[7]

Servanthood starts in the mind. With a simple prayer of three words:

"Change *me*, Lord."

7

Portrait
of a Servant,
Part One

"What do you want to be when you grow up?"

That's a favorite question we enjoy asking children. And the answers we get usually are "a policeman" or "a nurse" or maybe "a fireman." Some kids are visionary. They answer "a movie star" or "a singer" or "a doctor" or "a professional ball player." One recently told me he wanted to be either a car mechanic or a garbage collector. When I asked why, he gave the classic answer for a nine-year-old: *"So I can get dirty!"* I smiled as I had a flashback to my own childhood. And I understood.

Let's take that same question and ask it another way. Let's imagine asking Jesus Christ what He wants us to be when we grow up. Suddenly, it's a whole new question. I honestly believe He would give the same answer to every one of us: "I want you to be different . . . to be a servant." In all my life I cannot recall anybody ever saying that when he grew up he wanted to be a servant.

It sounds lowly . . . humiliating . . . lacking in dignity.

In his helpful book, *Honesty, Morality, & Conscience,* Jerry White talks about the concept of serving others.

> Christians are to be servants of both God and people. But most of us approach business and work—and life in general—with the attitude "What can I *get?*" rather than "What can I *give?*"

> We find it encouraging to think of ourselves as God's servants. Who would not want to be a servant of the King? But when it comes to serving other people, we begin to question the consequences. We feel noble when serving God; we feel humble when serving people. Serving God receives a favorable response; serving people, especially those who cannot repay, has no visible benefit or glory from anyone—except from God! Christ gave us the example: "The Son of Man did not come to be served, but to serve, and to give His life as a ransom for many" (Matt. 20:28). To be a servant of God we must be a servant of people.

> In business and work the concept of serving people must undergird all that we do. When we serve we think first of the one we are trying to serve. An employee who serves honestly in his work honors God and deepens his value to his employer. On the other hand, the self-serving employee will seldom be valued in any company.[1]

JESUS' COMMAND: "BE DIFFERENT!"

When Jesus walked the earth, He attracted a number of people to Himself. On one occasion, He sat down among them and taught them some bottom-line truths about how He wanted them to grow up. The scriptural account of His "Sermon on the Mount" is found in Matthew 5, 6, and 7. If I were asked to suggest an overall theme of this grand sermon, it would be—"Be different!" Time and again He states the way things were among the religious types of their day, and then He instructs them to be different. For example:

Matthew 5:21–22: "You have heard . . . but I say to you. . . ."

Matthew 5:27–28: "You have heard . . . but I say to you. . . ."

Matthew 5:33–34: "Again, you have heard . . . but I say to you. . . ."

Matthew 5:38–39: "You have heard . . . but I say to you. . . ."

Matthew 5:43–44: "You have heard . . . but I say to you. . . ."

In Matthew 6, He further explains how they were to be different when they gave to the needy (6:2), and when they prayed (6:5) and when they fasted (6:16). The key verse in the entire sermon is, *"Therefore, do not be like them . . ."* (6:8). You see, Jesus saw through all the pride and hypocrisy of others and was determined to instill in His disciples character traits of humility and authenticity. His unique teaching cut through the façade of religion like a sharp knife through warm butter. It remains to this day the most comprehensive delineation in all the New Testament of the Christian counterculture . . . offering a lifestyle totally at variance with the world system.

In the introduction of Jesus' sermon, doubtlessly the most familiar section is found in Matthew 5:1–12. Commonly called "The Beatitudes," this section is the most descriptive word-portrait of a servant ever recorded.

THE BEATITUDES: THREE OBSERVATIONS

Let's reread these immortal words slowly:

And when He saw the multitudes, He went up on the mountain; and after He sat down, His disciples came to Him.

And opening His mouth He began to teach them, saying, "Blessed are the poor in spirit, for theirs is the kingdom of heaven.

"Blessed are those who mourn, for they shall be comforted.

"Blessed are the gentle, for they shall inherit the earth.

"Blessed are those who hunger and thirst for righteousness, for they shall be satisfied.

"Blessed are the merciful, for they shall receive mercy.

"Blessed are the pure in heart, for they shall see God.

"Blessed are the peacemakers, for they shall be called sons of God.

"Blessed are those who have been persecuted for the sake of righteousness, for theirs is the kingdom of heaven.

"Blessed are you when men revile you, and persecute you, and say all kinds of evil against you falsely, on account of Me.

"Rejoice, and be glad, for your reward in heaven is great, for so they persecuted the prophets who were before you" (Matt. 5:1–12).

Let me suggest three general observations:

1. **These are eight character traits that identify true servant-hood.** When all eight are mixed together in a life, balance emerges. It is helpful to realize this is not a "multiple choice" list where we are free to pick and choose our favorites. Our Savior has stated very clearly those qualities that lead to a different lifestyle which pleases Him. A close examination of each is therefore essential.

2. **These traits open the door to inner happiness.** Here are the fundamental attitudes which, when pursued and experienced, bring great satisfaction. Jesus offers fulfillment here like nothing else on earth. Study how each begins: "Blessed are. . . ." This is the only time our Lord repeated the same term eight times consecutively. J. B. Phillips' translation picks up the thought correctly as he renders it "How happy" and "Happy." Those who enter into these attitudes find lasting happiness.

3. **Attached to each character trait is a corresponding promise.** Did you notice this? "Blessed are . . . (the trait) for . . ." (the promise). Christ holds out a particular benefit for each particular quality. And what great promises they are! Small wonder when He finished the sermon we read:

> The result was . . . the multitudes were amazed at His teaching; for He was teaching them as one having authority, and not as their scribes (Matt. 7:28–29).

Never before had His audience heard such marvelous truths presented in such an interesting and meaningful manner. They longed to have those promises incarnate in their lives. So do we.

An Analysis of Four Beatitudes

So much for the survey. Let's get specific. Rather than hurrying through all eight in a superficial manner, let's work our way through these first four qualities with care. We'll look at the next four in chapter 8. We shall be able to understand both the subtle shading and the rich color of the portrait painted by Jesus for all to appreciate and apply if we take our time and think through each servant characteristic.

"The Poor in Spirit"

At first glance, this seems to refer to those who have little or no money—people of poverty with zero financial security. Wrong. You'll note He speaks of being ". . . poor in spirit . . ." (italics mine). One helpful authority, William Barclay, clarifies the meaning:

> These words in Hebrew underwent a four-stage development of meaning. (i) They began by meaning simply *poor*. (ii) They went on to mean, *because poor, therefore having no influence or power, or help, or prestige.* (iii) They went on to mean, *because having no influence, therefore down-trodden and oppressed by men.* (iv) Finally, they came to describe *the man who, because he has no earthly resources whatever, puts his whole trust in God.* So in Hebrew the word *poor* was used to describe the humble and the helpless man who put his whole trust in God.[2]

This is an attitude of absolute, unvarnished humility. What an excellent way to begin the servant's portrait! It is the portrait of one who sees himself/herself as spiritually bankrupt, deserving of nothing . . . who turns to Almighty God in total trust.

Augustus M. Toplady caught a glimpse of this attitude when he wrote these words that became a part of the church's hymnody:

> Nothing in my hand I bring,
> Simply to Thy cross I cling;
> Naked, come to Thee for dress,
> Helpless, look to Thee for grace;
> Foul, I to the fountain fly,
> Wash me, Saviour, or I die![3]

This spirit of humility is very rare in our day of strong-willed, proud-as-a-peacock attitudes. The clinched fist has replaced the bowed head. The big mouth and the surly stare now dominate the scene once occupied by the quiet godliness of the "poor in spirit." How self-righteous we have become! How confident in and of ourselves! And with that attitude, how desperately unhappy we are! Christ Jesus offers genuine, lasting happiness to those whose hearts willingly declare:

> Oh, Lord
> I am a shell full of dust,
>   but animated with an invisible rational soul
>   and made anew by an unseen power of grace;
> Yet I am no rare object of valuable price,
>   but one that has nothing and is nothing,
>   although chosen of thee from eternity,
>   given to Christ, and born again;
> I am deeply convinced of the evil and misery of a
>   sinful state,
>   of the vanity of creatures,
>   but also of the sufficiency of Christ.
> When thou wouldst guide me I control myself,
> When thou wouldst be sovereign I rule myself.
> When thou wouldst take care of me I suffice myself.
> When I should depend on thy providings I supply
>   myself,
> When I should submit to thy providence I follow
>   my will,
> When I should study, love, honour, trust thee, I
>   serve myself

I fault and correct thy laws to suit myself,
Instead of thee I look to man's approbation,
   and am by nature an idolater.
Lord, it is my chief design to bring my heart
   back to thee.
Convince me that I cannot be my own god, or make
   myself happy,
   nor my own Christ to restore my joy,
   nor my own Spirit to teach, guide, rule me.
Help me to see that grace does this by providential
   affliction,
     for when my credit is god thou dost cast me
       lower,
     when riches are my idol thou dost wing them
       away,
     when pleasure is my all thou dost turn it
       into bitterness.
Take away my roving eye, curious ear, greedy appetite,
   lustful heart;
Show me that none of these things
   can heal a wounded conscience,
   or support a tottering frame,
   or uphold a departing spirit.
Then take me to the cross and leave me there.[4]

A special promise follows the trait of spiritual helplessness:
". . . for theirs is the kingdom of heaven," says Jesus. The
indispensable condition of receiving a part in the kingdom of
heaven is acknowledging our spiritual poverty. The person with
a servant's heart—not unlike a child trusting completely in his
parent's provision—is promised a place in Christ's kingdom.
The *opposite* attitude is clearly revealed in that Laodicean
congregation, where Christ rebuked them with severe words.
They were so proud, they were blind to their own selfishness:

I know your deeds, that you are neither cold nor hot; I would
that you were cold or hot.
So because you are lukewarm, and neither hot nor cold, I will
spit you out of My mouth.

Because you say, "I am rich, and have become wealthy, and have need of nothing," and you do not know that you are wretched and miserable and poor and blind and naked (Rev. 3:15–17).

Chances are good that there wasn't a servant in the whole lot at Laodicea.

First and foremost in the life of an authentic servant is a deep, abiding dependency on the living Lord. On the basis of that attitude, the kingdom of heaven is promised.

"Those Who Mourn"

Matthew, in recording Christ's teaching, chose the strongest Greek term in all his vocabulary when he wrote *mourn*. It is a heavy word—a passionate lament for one who was loved with profound devotion. It conveys the sorrow of a broken heart, the ache of soul, the anguished mind. It could include several scenes:

- Mourning over wrong in the world
- Mourning over personal loss
- Mourning over one's own wrong and sinfulness
- Mourning over the death of someone close.

Interestingly, this particular term also includes compassion, a sincere caring for others. Perhaps a satisfactory paraphrase would read: "How happy are those who care intensely for the hurts and sorrows and losses of others. . . ." At the heart of this character trait is COMPASSION, another servant attitude so desperately needed today.

Several years ago one of the men in our church fell while taking an early morning shower. As he slipped on the slick floor he fell against a sheet of glass with all his weight. The splintering glass stabbed deeply into his arm at and around his bicep. Blood spurted all over the bathroom. Paramedics arrived quickly with lights flashing, sirens screaming, and the "squawk box" blaring from within the cab. The man was placed on a stretcher as the family hurriedly raced against time to get him to the emergency ward nearby. Thankfully, his life was saved and he has fully recovered.

As I spoke with his wife about the ordeal, she told me not one neighbor even looked out his door, not to mention stopping by to see if they needed help. Not one . . . then or later. They showed no compassion by their lack of "mutual mourning." How unlike our Savior! We are told that:

> . . . we do not have a high priest who cannot sympathize with our weaknesses, but one who has been tempted in all things as we are, yet without sin (Heb. 4:15).

True servants are like their Lord, compassionate.

And the promise for those who "mourn"? The Savior promises ". . . they shall be comforted." In return, comfort will be theirs to claim. I find it significant that no mention is made of the source or the channel. Simply, it *will* come. Perhaps from the same one the servant cared for back when there was a need. It is axiomatic—there can be little comfort where there has been no grief.

Thus far we've found two attitudes in true servants—extreme dependence and strong compassion. There is more, much more.

"The Gentle"

The third character trait Jesus includes in His portrait of a servant is gentleness. *"Blessed are the gentle, for they shall inherit the earth"* (v. 5).

Immediately, we may get a false impression. We think, "Blessed are the weak for they shall become doormats." In our rough-and-rugged individualism, we think of gentleness as weakness, being soft, and virtually spineless. Not so! The Greek term is extremely colorful, helping us grasp a correct understanding of why the Lord sees the need for servants to be gentle.

It is used several ways in extrabiblical literature:

• A wild stallion that has been tamed, brought under control, is described as being "gentle."

· Carefully chosen words that soothe strong emotions are referred to as "gentle" words.

· Ointment that takes the fever and sting out of a wound is called "gentle."

· In one of Plato's works, a child asks the physician to be tender as he treats him. The child uses this term "gentle."

· Those who are polite, who have tact and are courteous, and who treat others with dignity and respect are called "gentle" people.

So then, gentleness includes such enviable qualities as having strength under control, being calm and peaceful when surrounded by a heated atmosphere, emitting a soothing effect on those who may be angry or otherwise beside themselves, and possessing tact and gracious courtesy that causes others to retain their self-esteem and dignity. Clearly, it includes a Christlikeness, since the same word is used to describe His own makeup:

Come to Me, all who are weary and heavy laden, and I will give you rest.
Take My yoke upon you, and learn from Me, for I am gentle and humble in heart; and YOU SHALL FIND REST FOR YOUR SOULS (Matt. 11:28–29).

And what does the promise mean ". . . *for they shall inherit the earth"*? It can be understood as one of two ways—now or later. Either "they will ultimately win out in this life" or "they will be given vast territories in the kingdom, to judge and to rule." Instead of losing, the gentle *gain*. Instead of being ripped off and taken advantage of, they come out ahead! David mentions this in one of his greatest psalms (37:7–11):

Rest in the Lord and wait patiently for Him;
Fret not yourself because of him who prospers in his way,
Because of the man who carries out wicked schemes.
Cease from anger, and forsake wrath;
Fret not yourself, it leads only to evildoing.
For evildoers will be cut off,
But those who wait for the Lord, they will inherit the land.

Yet a little while and the wicked man will be no more;
And you will look carefully for his place, and he will not be there.
But the humble will inherit the land,
And will delight themselves in abundant prosperity.

See the contrast?

From all outward appearance it seems as though the wicked win out. They prosper in their way, their schemes work, their cheating and lying and unfair treatment of others appear to pay off. They just seem to get richer and become more and more powerful. As James Russell Lowell once put it:

> Truth forever on the scaffold
> Wrong forever on the throne.

But God says it won't be "forever." The ultimate victory will *not* be won by the wicked. "The gentle" will win. Believe that, servant-in-the-making! Be different from the system! Stay on the scaffold . . . trust your heavenly Father to keep His promise regarding your inheritance. It is you who will be blessed.

Before closing this chapter, I want us to consider another character trait of a servant—the fourth in the list of eight.

"Those Who Hunger and Thirst for Righteousness"

The true servant possesses an insatiable appetite for what is right, a passionate drive for justice. Spiritually speaking, the servant is engaged in a pursuit of God . . . a hot, restless, eager longing to walk with Him, to please Him.

Eleventh-century Bernard of Clairveaux expressed it in this way in his hymn, *Jesus, Thou Joy of Loving Hearts:*

> We taste Thee, O Thou living Bread,
> And long to feast upon Thee still;
> We drink of Thee, the Fountain-
> head,
> And thirst our souls from Thee to fill.[5]

Bernard's pen dripped with that insatiable appetite for God. But there is a practical side of this fourth beatitude as well. It includes not just looking upward, pursuing a vertical holiness, but also looking around and being grieved over the corruption, the inequities, the gross lack of integrity, the moral compromises that abound. The servant "hungers and thirsts" for right on earth. Unwilling simply to sigh and shrug off the lack of justice and purity as inevitable, servants press on for righteousness. Some would call them idealists or dreamers.

One such person was Dag Hammarskjöld, former Secretary General of the United Nations, who died in a tragic airplane crash while flying over northern Rhodesia on a mission to negotiate a cease fire. In his fine book, *Markings*, the late statesman wrote:

> Hunger is my native place in the land of the passions. Hunger for fellowship, hunger for righteousness—for a fellowship founded on righteousness, and a righteousness attained in fellowship.
>
> Only life can satisfy the demands of life. And this hunger of mine can be satisfied for the simple reason that the nature of life is such that I can realize my individuality by becoming a bridge for others, a stone in the temple of righteousness.
>
> Don't be afraid of yourself, live your individuality to the full— but for the good of others. Don't copy others in order to buy fellowship, or make convention your law instead of living the righteousness.
>
> To become free and responsible. For this alone was man created. . . .[6]

And what will happen when this passionate appetite is a part of one's life? What does Jesus promise?

. . . *they shall be satisfied.*

A. T. Robertson, a Greek scholar of yesteryear, suggests the term *satisfied* is commonly used for feeding and fattening cattle, since it is derived from the term for fodder or grass.[7] What a picture of contentment! Like well-fed, hefty livestock . . . contented in soul and satisfied within, the servant with an appetite for righteousness will be filled. It's comforting to hear that promise. Normally, one would think such an insatiable pursuit would make one so intense there would be only fretfulness and agitation. But, no, Jesus promises to bring a satisfaction to such hungry and thirsty souls . . . a "rest" of spirit that conveys quiet contentment.

PRELIMINARY SUMMARY AND QUESTIONS

We are only halfway through the list, but it's a good place to stop and summarize what we have seen in this inspired portrait thus far. Jesus is describing how to be different, how to be His unique servant in a hostile, wicked world. He honors particular character traits and offers special rewards for each.

1. Those who are genuinely humble before God, who turn to Him in absolute dependence, will be assured of a place in His kingdom.

2. Those who show compassion on behalf of the needy, the hurting, will receive (in return) much comfort in their own lives.

3. Those who are gentle—strong within yet controlled without, who bring a soothing graciousness into irritating situations—will win out.

4. Those who have a passionate appetite for righteousness, both heavenly and earthly, will receive from the Lord an unusual measure of personal contentment and satisfaction.

Before examining the final four character traits of a servant in the next chapter, let's ask ourselves these questions (try to answer each one directly and honestly):

· Am I really different!

· Do I take all this seriously . . . so much so that I am willing to change?

· Is it coming through to me that serving others is one of the most Christlike attitudes I can have?

· What significant difference will the ideas expressed in this chapter have on my life?

The bottom-line question is not "What do you want to be when you grow up?" but "What are you becoming, now that you're grown?"

8

Portrait
of a Servant,
Part Two

Y ou don't run through an art gallery; you walk very slowly. You often stop, study the treasured works of art, taking the time to appreciate what has been painted. You examine the texture, the technique, the choice and mixture of colors, the subtle as well as the bold strokes of the brush, the shadings. And the more valuable the canvas, the more time and thought it deserves. You may even return to it later for a further and deeper look, especially if you are a student of that particular artist.

In the gallery of His priceless work, the Lord God has included a portrait of vast value. It is the portrait of a servant carefully painted in words that take time to understand and appreciate. The frame in which the portrait has been placed is Jesus Christ's immortal Sermon on the Mount. We have examined a portion of the portrait already, but we are returning for another look, hoping to see more that will help us become the kind of persons the Artist has portrayed.

ANALYSIS OF FOUR MORE QUALITIES

In His word-portrait of a servant, Christ emphasizes eight characteristics or qualities. We have studied the first four in the previous chapter. We now return to the picture for an analysis of the final four.

> Blessed are the merciful, for they shall receive mercy.
> Blessed are the pure in heart, for they shall see God.
> Blessed are the peacemakers, for they shall be called sons of God.
> Blessed are those who have been persecuted for the sake of righteousness, for theirs is the kingdom of heaven.
> Blessed are you when men revile you, and persecute you, and say all kinds of evil against you falsely, on account of Me.
> Rejoice, and be glad, for your reward in heaven is great, for so they persecuted the prophets who were before you (Matt. 5:7–12).

"The Merciful"

Mercy is concern for people in need. It is ministry to the miserable. Offering help for those who hurt . . . who suffer under the distressing blows of adversity and hardship. The term itself has an interesting background.

> It does not mean only to sympathise with a person in the popular sense of the term; it does not mean simply to feel sorry for someone in trouble. *Chesedh, mercy,* means the ability to get right inside the other person's skin. . . . Clearly this is much more than an emotional wave of pity; clearly this demands a quite deliberate effort of the mind and of the will. It denotes a sympathy which is not given, as it were, from outside, but which comes from a deliberate identification with the other person, until we see things as he sees them, and feel things as he feels them.[1]

Those special servants of God who extend mercy to the miserable often do so with much encouragement because they identify with the sorrowing—they "get inside their skin." Rather than watching from a distance or keeping the needy safely at arm's length, they get in touch, involved, and offer assistance that alleviates some of the pain.

A large group of the collegians in our church in Fullerton, California, pile into our bus one weekend a month and travel together—not to a mountain resort or the beach for fun-n-games, but to a garbage dump in Tijuana, Mexico, where hundreds of poverty-stricken Mexican families live. Our young adults, under the encouraging leadership of Kenneth Kemp (one of our pastoral staff team members), bring apples and other foodstuff plus money they have collected to share with those in that miserable existence. There are times when the students can hardly believe what they see and hear *and smell* as they witness raw, unmasked poverty in the garbage dump at Tijuana.

What are they doing? They are showing mercy . . . a ministry to others that is born out of the womb of identification. In our isolated, cold society, mercy is rarely demonstrated. Shocking stories make headlines today with remarkable regularity.

A young woman was brutally attacked as she returned to her apartment late one night. She screamed and shrieked as she fought for her life . . . yelling until she was hoarse . . . for thirty minutes . . . as she was beaten and abused. Thirty-eight people watched the half-hour episode in rapt fascination from their windows. Not one so much as walked over to the telephone and called the police. She died that night as thirty-eight witnesses stared in silence.

Another's experience was similar. Riding on a subway, a seventeen-year-old youth was quietly minding his own business when he was stabbed repeatedly in the stomach by attackers. Eleven riders watched the stabbing, but none came to assist the young man. Even after the thugs had fled and the train had pulled out of the station and he lay there in a pool of his own blood, not one of the eleven came to his side.

Less dramatic, but equally shocking, was the ordeal of a lady in New York City. While shopping on Fifth Avenue in busy Manhattan, this lady tripped and broke her leg. Dazed, anguished, and in shock, she called out for help. Not for two minutes. Not for twenty minutes. But for *forty* minutes, as shoppers and business executives, students and merchants walked around her and stepped over her, completely ignoring her cries. After literally hundreds had passed by, a cab driver finally pulled over, hauled her into his taxi, and took her to a local hospital.

> If you had a friend who is in need . . . and you say to him, "Well, good-bye and God bless you; stay warm and eat hearty," and then don't give him clothes or food, what good does that do? (James 2:15–16, TLB).

The apostle John probes even deeper when he asks:

> . . . if someone who is supposed to be a Christian . . . sees a brother in need, and won't help him—how can God's love be within him? (1 John 3:17, TLB).

True servants are merciful. They care. They get involved. They get dirty, if necessary. They offer more than pious words.

And what do they get in return? What does Christ promise? *". . . they shall receive mercy."* Those who remain detached, distant, and disinterested in others will receive like treatment. But God promises that those who reach out and demonstrate mercy will, in turn, receive it. Both from other people as well as from God Himself. We could paraphrase this beatitude: "O the bliss of one who identifies with and assists others in need—who gets inside their skin so completely he sees with their eyes and thinks with their thoughts and feels with their feelings. The one who does that will find that others do the same for him when he is in need."

That is exactly what Jesus, our Savior, did for us when He came to earth. By becoming human. He got right inside our skin, literally. That made it possible for Him to see life through our eyes, feel the sting of our pain, and identify with the anguish of human need. He understands. Remember those great words:

But Jesus the Son of God is our great High Priest who has gone to heaven itself to help us; therefore let us never stop trusting him. This High Priest of ours understands our weaknesses, since he had the same temptations we do, though he never once gave way to them and sinned (Heb. 4:14–15, TLB).

"The Pure in Heart"

Like the first characteristic—"poor in spirit" (v. 3)—this quality emphasizes the inner man . . . the motive . . . the "heart." It does not refer simply to doing the right things, but doing the right things *for the right reason*. Being free from duplicity, hypocrisy, and/or sham. God desires His servants to be "real" people—authentic to the core. The portrait He paints is realistic.

In Jesus' day many of the religious authorities who claimed to serve the people were not "pure in heart." Far from it! Hypocritical and phony, they played a role that lacked internal integrity. In Matthew 23—one of the most severe rebukes against hypocrisy in all the Bible—we find words in strong contrast with the beatitudes. Instead of eight "Blessed are yous," there are eight "Woe unto yous." Count them—Matthew 23:13, 14, 15, 16, 23, 25, 27, and 29!

Woe unto whom? Well, read verses 25–28.

> Woe to you, scribes and Pharisees, hypocrites! For you clean the outside of the cup and of the dish, but inside they are full of robbery and self-indulgence.
>
> You blind Pharisee, first clean the inside of the cup and of the dish, so that the outside of it may become clean also.
>
> Woe to you, scribes and Pharisees, hypocrites! For you are like whitewashed tombs which on the outside appear beautiful, but inside they are full of dead men's bones and all uncleanness.
>
> Even so you too outwardly appear righteous to men, but inwardly you are full of hypocrisy and lawlessness.

Wow, *Jesus* said that! It is doubtful He despised anything among those who claimed to serve God more than hypocrisy—a lack of purity of heart. Did you notice what characterized the phony Pharisees?

· They were big on rules and little on godliness.
· They were big on externals and little on internals.
· They were big on public commands and little on personal obedience.
· They were big on appearance and little on reality.

On the outside they "appeared righteous to men," but inwardly they were "full of dead men's bones . . . full of hypocrisy." Why did He hate that so much? Because it represented the antithesis of servanthood. Time after time, therefore, He announced, "Woe to you. . . !"

Back to Matthew 5:8—the "pure in heart." Jesus extols this virtue. The term *pure* literally means "clean." It's the idea of being uncontaminated, without corruption or alloy. Without guile . . . sincere and honest in motive.

I love the story of the well-respected British pastor who, many years ago, took the trolley early Monday morning from his home in the suburbs to his church in the downtown section of London. He paid the driver as he got on, preoccupied with his busy schedule and the needs of his large congregation. It wasn't until he was seated that he realized the driver had given him too much change. Fingering the coins, his first thought was an alien one, "My, how wonderfully God provides!" But the longer he sat there, the less comfortable he became. His conscience telegraphed a strong signal of conviction within him. As he walked to the door to get off near his parish, he looked at the driver and quietly said, "When I got on, you accidentally gave me too much change."

The driver, with a wry smile, replied, "It was no accident at all. You see, I was in your congregation yesterday and heard your sermon on honesty. I just thought I'd put you to the test, Reverend."

Christ promises that consistent servants who are pure in heart "shall see God." There is no doubt about the destiny of these individuals. For sure, some glorious day in the future, these servants will see the Lord and hear the most significant words that will ever enter human ears: ". . . Well done, good and faithful slave; you were faithful . . . enter into the joy of your master" (Matt. 25:21).

Before we move on to the next servant quality, let me challenge you to become "pure in heart." Think about what it would mean, what changes you would have to make, what habits you'd have to break . . . most of all, what masks you'd have to peel off.

As I write these words, my family and I are spending Thanksgiving week high up in the Rockies at a ski resort in Keystone, Colorado. I was invited to speak to about five hundred single career people. Many of them are on the Campus Crusade for Christ staff. What a great bunch! All week I have been talking about servanthood (sound familiar?) and emphasizing being real, authentic, pure-in-heart people. We've discussed our tendency to cover up, to say one thing and mean another, to be downright hypocritical—yet in such a clever way that nobody knows it.

Last night I decided to try something I had never done before to drive the point home. At my last birthday my sister gave me a full-face rubber mask . . . one of those crazy things that slip over your entire head. She told me she'd give me ten dollars if I'd wear it into the pulpit one Sunday (my kids raised it to fifteen dollars), but I just couldn't do it! Well, last night I wore that ugly beast when I got up to speak. I figured if anybody could handle it, this gang could. *It was wild!*

I didn't call attention to it. Without any explanation, I just stood up and began to speak on being authentic. There I stood pressing on, making one statement after another as the place came apart at the seams. Why? Anybody knows why! My mask canceled out everything I had to say, especially on *that* subject. It's impossible to be very convincing while you wear a mask.

I finally pulled the thing off and the place settled down almost immediately. As soon as it did, everybody got the point. It's a funny thing, when we wear *literal* masks, nobody is fooled. But how easy it is to wear invisible ones and fake people out by the hundreds week after week. Did you know that the word *hypocrite* comes from the ancient Greek plays? An actor would place a large, grinning mask in front of his face and quote his comedy lines as the audience would roar with laughter. He would then slip backstage and grab a frowning, sad, oversized mask and come back quoting tragic lines as the audience would moan and weep. Guess what he was called. A *hupocritos*, one who wears a mask.

Servants who are "pure in heart" have peeled off their masks. And God places special blessing on their lives.

"The Peacemakers"

Interestingly, this is the only time in all the New Testament that the Greek term translated "peacemakers" appears. Maybe it will help us understand the meaning by pointing out first what it does *not* mean.

· It does not mean, "Blessed are those who avoid all conflict and confrontations."

· Neither does it mean, "Blessed are those who are laid back, easygoing, and relaxed."

· Nor, "Blessed are those who defend a 'peace at any price' philosophy."

· It doesn't mean, "Blessed are the passive, those who compromise their convictions when surrounded by those who would disagree."

No, none of those ideas are characteristics of the "peacemaker" in this verse.

The overall thrust of Scripture is the imperative, "Make peace!" Just listen:

If possible, so far as it depends on you, be at peace with all men (Rom. 12:18).

So then let us pursue the things which make for peace and the building up of one another (Rom. 14:19).

For where jealousy and selfish ambition exist, there is disorder and every evil thing.

But the wisdom from above is first pure, then peaceable, gentle, reasonable, full of mercy and good fruits, unwavering, without hypocrisy.

And the seed whose fruit is righteousness is sown in peace by those who make peace.

What is the source of quarrels and conflicts among you? Is not the source your pleasures that wage war in your members?

You lust and do not have; so you commit murder. And you are envious and cannot obtain; so you fight and quarrel (James 3:16–4:2).

Get the picture? A "peacemaker" is the servant who . . . First, is at peace with himself—internally, at ease . . . not agitated, ill-tempered, in turmoil . . . and therefore not abrasive. Second, he/she works hard to settle quarrels, not start them . . . is accepting, tolerant, finds no pleasure in being negative.

In the words of Ephesians 4:3, peacemakers ". . . preserve the unity of the Spirit in the bond of peace."

Ever been around Christians who are *not* peacemakers? Of course. Was it pleasant? Did you sense a servant's heart? Were you built up and encouraged . . . was the body of Christ strengthened and supported? You know the answers.

In Leslie Flynn's potent book *Great Church Fights* (I like that title), he does a masterful job of describing just how petty and abrasive we can become. He includes an anonymous poem that bites deeply into our rigid intolerance. Our tendency toward exclusiveness is exposed for all to see:

> Believe as I believe, no more, no less;
> That I am right, and no one else, confess;
> Feel as I feel, think only as I think;
> Eat what I eat, and drink but what I drink;
> Look as I look, do always as I do;
> And then, and only then, I'll fellowship with you. [2]
> —Source Unknown

Whoever lives by that philosophy does not qualify as a peacemaker, I can assure you.

But enough of the negative! Solomon gives us wise counsel on some of the things peacemakers do:

• **They build up.** "The wise woman builds her house . . ." (Prov. 14:1).

• **They watch their tongues and heal rather than hurt.** "A gentle answer turns away wrath . . ." (Prov. 15:1). "Pleasant words are a honeycomb, sweet to the soul and healing to the bones" (Prov. 16:24).

• **They are slow to anger.** "A hot-tempered man stirs up strife, but the slow to anger pacifies contention" (Prov. 15:18). "He who is slow to anger is better than the mighty, and he who rules his spirit, than who captures a city" (Prov. 16:32).

• **They are humble and trusting.** "An arrogant man stirs up strife, but he who trusts in the lord will prosper" (Prov. 28:25).

The Lord Jesus states a marvelous promise that peacemakers can claim: ". . . they shall be called sons of God." God's children. Few things are more godlike than *peace*. When we promote it, pursue it, model it, we are linked directly with Him.

A man I have admired for two decades, the man who taught me Hebrew in seminary many years ago, is Dr. Bruce Waltke. He is not only a Semitic scholar *par excellence*, he is a gracious servant of our Lord. In my opinion, he is one of the finest examples of a peacemaker in the family of God. Too brilliant for words, yet the epitome of grace and love. What a magnificent balance!

A number of years ago, Dr. Waltke, another pastor, a graduate student at Brandeis University (also a seminary graduate), and I toured the mother church of the First Church of Christ Scientist in downtown Boston. The four of us were completely anonymous to the elderly lady who smiled as we entered. She had no idea she was meeting four evangelical ministers—and we chose not to identify ourselves, at least at first.

She showed us several interesting things on the main floor. When we got to the multiple-manual pipe organ, she began to talk about their doctrine and especially their belief about no judgment in the life beyond. Dr. Waltke waited for just the right moment and very casually asked:

"But, Ma'am, doesn't it say somewhere in the Bible 'It is appointed unto man once to die and after that, the judgment'?" He could have quoted Hebrews 9:27 in Greek! But he was so gracious, so tactful with the little lady. I must confess, I stood back thinking, "Go for it, Bruce. Now we've got her where we want her!"

The lady, without a pause, said simply, "Would you like to see the second floor?"

You know what Dr. Waltke said? "We surely would, thank you."

She smiled, somewhat relieved, and started to lead us up a flight of stairs.

I couldn't believe it! All I could think was, "No, don't let her get away. Make her answer your question!" As I was wrestling within, I pulled on the scholar's arm and said in a low voice, "Hey, why didn't you nail the lady? Why didn't you press the point and not let her get away until she answered?"

Quietly and calmly he put his hand on my shoulder and whispered, "But, Chuck, that wouldn't have been fair. That wouldn't have been very loving, either—now would it?"

Wham! The quiet rebuke left me reeling. I shall never forget that moment. And to complete the story, you'll be interested to know that in less than twenty minutes he was sitting with the woman alone, tenderly and carefully speaking with her about the Lord Jesus Christ. She sat in rapt attention. He, the gracious peacemaker, had won a hearing. And I, the scalp-snatcher, had learned an unforgettable lesson.

Do you know what she saw in my friend? A living representation of one of God's sons . . . exactly as God promised in his beatitude . . . *"they shall be called sons of God."*

In this chapter we have been examining a portrait. We have seen the servant as merciful, authentic, and one who actively pursues peace. There remains one final part of the picture we need to linger over and appreciate.

"Those Who Have Been Persecuted"

I don't know how this strikes you, but it seems misplaced at first glance. Especially on the heels of what we just learned about being peacemakers. But it is not misplaced. Realistically, wrong treatment often comes upon those who do what is *right*. I deal with this at length in chapter 12. We who genuinely desire to serve others soon discover that being mistreated isn't the exception. It's the rule! Christ knew that was so. Read the verses carefully.

> Blessed are those who have been persecuted for the sake of righteousness, for theirs is the kingdom of heaven.
> Blessed are you when men revile you, and persecute you, and say all kinds of evil against you falsely, on account of Me.
> Rejoice, and be glad, for your reward in heaven is great, for so they persecuted the prophets who were before you (Matt. 5:10–12).

Did you notice something? Not "if" men revile you . . . but "when" they revile you. And not only will they revile you, they will persecute you and say all kinds of evil against you—lies and slanderous accusations. Clearly, Jesus is speaking of being viciously mistreated. It's tough to bear! But the Savior says you will be "blessed" when you endure it—promising a great reward for your patient, mature endurance. There are times when the only way servants can make it through such severe times without becoming bitter is by focusing on the ultimate rewards that are promised. Jesus even says we are to "rejoice and be glad" as we think on the great rewards He will give to us in heaven.

Charles Haddon Spurgeon remains one of the most colorful and gifted preachers in the history of the church. Any man who loves to preach and desires to cultivate the art and skill of communication must study Spurgeon. Before the man was thirty, he was the most popular preacher in England. The new Tabernacle was filled to overflowing every Lord's Day as people came miles by horse and buggy to hear the gifted man handle the Word of God. They were challenged, encouraged, exhorted, fed, and built up in the Christian faith. He was truly a phenomenon. As a result, he became the object of great criticism by the press, by other pastors, by influential people in London, and by petty parishioners. The man, not always a model of quiet piety (to say the least), had numerous enemies. Normally, he handled the criticism fairly well . . . but finally it began to get to him. He began to slump beneath the attacks. The persecution started to take a severe toll on his otherwise resilient spirit.

I am told that his wife, seeing the results of those verbal blows on her husband, decided to assist him in getting back on his feet and regaining his powerful stature in the pulpit. She found in her Bible Matthew 5:10–12—the beatitude we have been studying—and she printed in beautiful old English the words of this passage on a large sheet of paper. Then she tacked that sheet to the ceiling of their bedroom, directly above Charles' side of the bed! Every morning, every evening, when he would rest his enormous frame in his bed, the words were there to meet and to encourage him.

> Blessed are those who have been persecuted for the sake of righteousness, for theirs is the kingdom of heaven.
> Blessed are you when men revile you, and persecute you, and say all kinds of evil against you falsely, on account of Me.
> Rejoice, and be glad, for your reward in heaven is great, for so they persecuted the prophets who were before you.

The large sheet of paper remained fixed to the ceiling for an extended period of time until it had done the job. May Mrs. Spurgeon's tribe increase! It is refreshing to think how a marriage partner can be such a vital channel of encouragement.

And it is also encouraging to see that we have no corner on the problem of persecution. Did you observe what Christ said? ". . . so they persecuted the prophets who were before you." Servants, that statement will help us call a halt to the next pity party we are tempted to throw for ourselves. We are not alone. It has been going on for centuries.

A LAST LOOK AT THE PORTRAIT

Shortly before her death in February of 1971, my mother did an oil painting for me. It has become a silent "friend" of mine, a mute yet eloquent expression of my calling. It is a picture of a shepherd with his sheep. The man is standing all alone with his crook in his hand, facing the hillside with sheep here and there. You cannot see the shepherd's face, but the little woolies surrounding him have personalities all their own. Some have the appearance of being devoted and loving, one looks independent and stubborn, another is starting to wander in the distance. But the shepherd is there with his flock, faithfully and diligently tending them.

The rather large piece of art hangs in my study with a light above it. There are occasions when I am bone weary after a huge day of people demands, preaching, and close contact with the Fullerton flock. Occasionally on days like this, I will turn off my desk lamp and my light overhead and leave on only the light on that unique painting. It helps me keep my perspective. It is a reminder . . . a simple, silent affirmation that I am right where God wants me, doing the very things He wants me to do. There is something very encouraging about taking a final look at the shepherd with his sheep at the end of my day.

We have done that in these two chapters. With a close eye on details, we have studied a portrait Jesus painted of a servant. And we have found it to be both enlightening and encouraging. We have found His promises to be assuring and His repeated reminders ("Blessed are . . .") to be affirming. He has described our calling by explaining our role as:
- Poor in spirit
- Mourning
- Gentle
- Hungering and thirsting for righteousness
- Merciful
- Pure in heart
- Peacemakers
- Persecuted.

As we have turned out all the other lights that distract us, it has helped to concentrate our full attention on these eight specifics. The question we now must face is: Can such a person as this really influence a stubborn, competitive, strong-willed world? Is it possible for servants to make an impact?

The next chapter offers a resounding "Yes!" In our tasteless, dark world, servants actually become the only source of salt and light.

9

The Influence of a Servant

Ours is a tough, rugged, wicked world. Aggression, rebellion, violence, cutthroat competition, and retaliation abound. Not just internationally, but personally. What is true in the secret council chambers of nations is also true behind closed doors of homes. We are stubborn, warring people. "The American home," according to a study completed at the University of Rhode Island, is described as "the most dangerous place to be, outside of riots and a war!"[1] No less than 30 percent of all American couples experience some form of domestic violence in their lifetimes. This helps explain why 20 percent of all police officers killed in the line of duty are killed while answering calls involving family fights, and why it is estimated that anywhere from six to fifteen *million* women are battered in our nation each year.[2] And the figures are on the increase. The heart of mankind is totally and unashamedly depraved!

What possible influence could the servants described in Matthew 5:1–12 have on a hard, hostile society like ours? What impact—how much clout—do the "poor in spirit," the "gentle," the "merciful," the "pure in heart," or the "peacemakers" actually have? Such feeble-sounding virtues seem about as influential as pillow fighting in a nuclear war. Especially with the odds stacked against us. Servants of Jesus Christ will always be in the minority . . . a small remnant surrounded by a strong-minded majority with their fists clenched. Can our presence do much good? Isn't it pretty much a wasted effort?

Jesus—the One who first painted the servant's portrait—did not share this skepticism. But neither did He deny the battle. Don't forget the final touches He put on that inspired canvas, which we just examined and admired. Remember these words? They make it clear that society is a combat zone not a vacation spot.

> Blessed are those who have been persecuted for the sake of righteousness, for theirs is the kingdom of heaven.
> Blessed are you when men revile you, and persecute you, and say all kinds of evil against you falsely, on account of Me.
> Rejoice, and be glad, for your reward in heaven is great, for so they persecuted the prophets who were before you (Matt. 5:10–12).

No, He never promised us a rose garden. He came up front with us and admitted that the arena of this world is not a friend of grace to help us on to God. Nevertheless, strange as it may seem, He went on to tell that handful of Palestinian peasants (and *all* godly servants in every generation) that their influence would be nothing short of remarkable. They would be "the salt of the earth" and they would be "the light of the world." And so shall we! So far-reaching would be the influence of servants in society, their presence would be as significant as salt on food and as light on darkness. Neither is loud or externally impressive, but both are essential. Without our influence this old world would soon begin to realize our absence. Even though it may not admit it, society needs both salt and light.

KEEPER OF THE SPRING

The late Peter Marshall, an eloquent speaker and for several years the chaplain of the United States Senate, used to love to tell the story of "The Keeper of the Spring,"[3] a quiet forest dweller who lived high above an Austrian village along the eastern slopes of the Alps. The old gentleman had been hired many years ago by a young town council to clear away the debris from the pools of water up in the mountain crevices that fed the lovely spring flowing through their town. With faithful, silent regularity, he patrolled the hills, removed the leaves and branches, and wiped away the silt that would otherwise choke and contaminate the fresh flow of water. By and by, the village became a popular attraction for vacationers. Graceful swans floated along the crystal clear spring, the millwheels of various businesses located near the water turned day and night, farmlands were naturally irrigated, and the view from restaurants was picturesque beyond description.

Years passed. One evening the town council met for its semiannual meeting. As they reviewed the budget, one man's eye caught the salary figure being paid the obscure keeper of the spring. Said the keeper of the purse, "Who is the old man? Why do we keep him on year after year? No one ever sees him. For all we know the strange ranger of the hills is doing us no good. He isn't necessary any longer!" By a unanimous vote, they dispensed with the old man's services.

For several weeks nothing changed. By early autumn the trees began to shed their leaves. Small branches snapped off and fell into the pools, hindering the rushing flow of sparkling water. One afternoon someone noticed a slight yellowish-brown tint in the spring. A couple days later the water was much darker. Within another week, a slimy film covered sections of the water along the banks and a foul odor was soon detected. The millwheels moved slower, some finally ground to a halt. Swans left as did the tourists. Clammy fingers of disease and sickness reached deeply into the village.

Quickly, the embarrassed council called a special meeting. Realizing their gross error in judgment, they hired back the old keeper of the spring . . . and within a few weeks the veritable river of life began to clear up. The wheels started to turn, and new life returned to the hamlet in the Alps once again.

Fanciful though it may be, the story is more than an idle tale. It carries with it a vivid, relevant analogy directly related to the times in which we live. What the keeper of the springs meant to the village, Christian servants mean to our world. The preserving, taste-giving bite of salt mixed with the illuminating, hope-giving ray of light may seem feeble and needless . . . but God help any society that attempts to exist without them! You see, the village without the Keeper of the Spring is a perfect representation of the world system without salt and light.

CRITICAL ESTIMATION OF OUR TIMES

To help describe just how hopeless and empty society really is, let's glance over 2 Timothy 3. Within the first thirteen verses, I find three undeniable descriptions of our world—difficult, depraved, and deceived.

Difficult

Read verses 1 through 7 very carefully.

> But realize this, that in the last days difficult times will come.
> For men will be lovers of self, lovers of money, boastful, arrogant, revilers, disobedient to parents, ungrateful, unholy, unloving, irreconcilable, malicious gossips, without self-control, brutal, haters of good, treacherous, reckless, conceited, lovers of pleasure rather than lovers of God; holding to a form of godliness, although they have denied its power; and avoid such men as these.
> For among them are those who enter into households and captivate weak women weighed down with sins, led on by various impulses, always learning and never able to come to the knowledge of the truth (2 Tim. 3:1–7).

Now, with your pen, go back up to the first verse and circle the term *difficult.* One version renders the word *perilous* (KJV). Another translates it *terrible* (NIV). The Greek root word meant "grievous, harsh, fierce, savage." It is used only one other time in the New Testament. In Matthew 8:28 it appears when the writer describes two men with demons as being "exceedingly violent." What an apt description of our world! Savage, harsh, violent. If you question that, if you need proof that that is no exaggeration, check this morning's newspaper or listen to the evening news. Both will convince you our "village" is in desperate straits.

Depraved

Now, look at the next two verses:

And just as Jannes and Jambres opposed Moses, so these men also oppose the truth, men of depraved mind, rejected as regards the faith.

But they will not make further progress; for their folly will be obvious to all, as also that of those two came to be (vv. 8–9).

Paul mentions two men from the days of Moses as representatives of people in these "difficult" times. *Depraved* is the word to describe them. Circle it in verse 8. It means mankind is as bad off spiritually as it can possibly be. Dead toward God. Unmoved by anything spiritual. Hard-hearted and dark within. Two sections out of Isaiah come to my mind as illustrations of human depravity.

All of us like sheep have gone astray,
Each of us has turned to his own way;
But the Lord has caused the iniquity of us all
To fall on Him (Isa. 53:6).

For all of us have become like one who is unclean,
And all our righteous deeds are like a filthy garment;
And all of us wither like a leaf,
And our iniquities, like the wind, take us away.

> And there is no one who calls on Thy name,
> Who arouses himself to take hold of Thee;
> For Thou hast hidden Thy face from us,
> And hast delivered us into the power of our iniquities (Isa. 64:6–7).

"All . . . all . . . all . . . all . . . all." Depravity is a universal disease in society. And we are reaping what we have sowed. Our world is on a collision course destined for a Christless eternity. Now let's look at the third descriptive term.

Deceived

It will not surprise you to read these words:

> But evil men and impostors will proceed from bad to worse, deceiving and being deceived (2 Tim. 3:13).

Circle that last word. The "village" is a place where impostors flourish. Rip-off experts flood every profession. Religious charlatans are here as well. Many politicians speak smoothly from both sides of their mouths. No one can deny the phony-baloney façade of ads and fads. And Scripture is right, it proceeds "from bad to worse." Remove "the spring" of life from the village—take away the salt and the light—and within a brief time "the village" becomes a diseased cesspool of contamination. Enter: the Keeper of the spring! He may seem removed and uninfluential, but without the salt and light He quietly provides, there is only hopeless despair.

Technically, there can be only one "Keeper of the Spring": Jesus Christ, the Lord. But we, His servants, His representative-ambassadors, have been commissioned to carry on in His absence. We, His servants, are assigned to the task not unlike the old gentleman in the Alps. But how can the job be done?

INDISPENSABLE INFLUENCES FOR GOOD

Let's turn again to Matthew 5. For the first twelve verses, you'll recall that Christ speaks of the character qualities of the servant. Interestingly, He uses *they, their,* and *those* throughout the verses. But when He applies the influence of servanthood on society, He says *you.* "*You* are the salt . . . *you* are the light." It is personal. Equally significant is the obvious lack of the words *like* or *as.* Salt and light are things we *are*, not things we represent, not what we provide or attempt to compare with ourselves. Here's the point: A society characterized by savage violence and the darkness of depravity and deception will, without salt and light, deteriorate and ultimately self-destruct. Because servants of Christ are both salt and light, our influence is essential for survival.

John R. W. Stott expresses the value of our influence this way:

> The world is evidently a dark place, with little or no light of its own, since an external source of light is needed to illumine it. True, it is "always talking about its enlightenment," but much of its boasted light is in reality darkness. The world also manifests a constant tendency to deteriorate. The notion is not that the world is tasteless and that Christians can make it less insipid ("The thought of making the world palatable to God is quite impossible"), but that it is putrifying. It cannot stop itself from going bad. Only salt introduced from outside can do this. The church, on the other hand, is set in the world with a double role, as salt to arrest—or at least to hinder—the process of social decay, and as light to dispel the darkness.
>
> When we look at the two metaphors more closely, we see that they are deliberately phrased in order to be parallel to each other. In each case Jesus first makes an affirmation ("You are the salt of the earth," "You are the light of the world"). Then he adds a rider, the condition on which the affirmation depends (the salt must retain its saltness, the light must be allowed to shine). Salt is good for nothing if its saltness is lost; light is good for nothing if it is concealed.[4]

As the servant's salt influences a putrifying society, a measure of preservation is provided. As the servant's light influences a depraved, dying society, a measure of darkness is dispelled. Let's probe a bit into these two metaphors.

The Salt of the Earth

Ever smelled old, rotten meat? Remember forgetting for several weeks something you put in the refrigerator? There is an odor that accompanies decay that's like nothing else. Down in Houston where I was raised, we were only fifty miles from the seaport city of Galveston. Delicious, fresh seafood was available in numerous restaurants in that area—and still is. But there were other ways we used to use seafood, especially shrimp. When a friend would get married, one of our favorite tricks was to secretly pull off the hubcaps of his getaway car and stuff them full of shrimp. It was great! Those shrimp wouldn't make any noise as they sloshed around hour after hour in the heat of South Texas. But the result was unreal. After two or three days of driving, parking in the sun, stop-and-go traffic, the bride (bless her shy heart) would slowly start sliding over closer to the door. She would begin to wonder if maybe her beloved groom had forgotten his Right Guard. As the day wore on, he would begin to wonder the same about her! All the while those little shrimp were doing their thing in each wheel. Finally (and sometimes they wouldn't discover the trick for over a week!), young Don Juan would pop off a hubcap—and I don't need to tell you the result. Old shrimp inside a hot hubcap for a week would make a skunk's spray seem like a shot of Chanel No. 5. *It is gross!* To keep shrimp, you must preserve them. If you don't, they perish. Years ago salt was used. Today we use ice more often.

Think of this earth as shrimp when you read these words:

> You are the salt of the earth; but if the salt has become tasteless, how will it be made salty again? It is good for nothing any more, except to be thrown out and trampled under foot by men (Matt. 5:13).

The earth and all its inhabitants are in a continual state of perishing. We are "salt to the world" (NEB). R.V.G. Tasker, professor emeritus of New Testament exegesis at the University of London, is correct: "The disciples, accordingly, are called to be a moral disinfectant in a world where moral standards are

low, constantly changing, or non-existent."⁵ Our very presence
halts corruption. Salt is also a healing agent. And it creates a
thirst. It adds flavor, increasing the delectable taste of most
foods. Salt is amazingly beneficial—*but*. Did you miss that little
word in verse 13? ". . . but if the salt has become tasteless. . . ." (meaning "if the salt has lost its bite, its unique-
ness"). Jesus introduces not an imaginary warning, but a real
one. Take away the Christian's distinctive contribution and
nothing of worthwhile value remains. We become "good for
nothing," exactly as the Lord put it.

I want to be quite direct with you. Secular thought has taken
a tragic toll on the servant of God's distinctiveness. This has
begun to influence the church of Jesus Christ. Many a believer
has surrendered his mind to the world system. The uniquely
Christian mind, therefore, is a rare find. Humanism, secularism,
intellectualism, and materialism have invaded our thinking
to such a marked degree our salt has become diluted—in
some cases, nonexistent. Francis Schaeffer, with prophetlike
zeal and determination, has attempted to awaken us to this
malady. One who could be called his British counterpart,
Harry Blamires (a man C. S. Lewis tutored at Oxford), comes
right out and dogmatically declares, "There is no longer a
Christian mind."⁶ Influenced and impressed by the press, our
secularized system of education, shallow social expectations, and
the quasi-omnipotent forces of conformity to peer pressure (not
to mention the impact of television and movies), Christian
servants can be easily caught in the trap. We can literally stop
thinking biblically and stop shaking salt.

This is why Jesus states His concern so forcefully—"It is good
for nothing any more, except to be thrown out and trampled
under foot by men" (Matt. 5:13). We must do a work of
preservation . . . or we lose our influence and become as
insignificant as a layer of dust on city streets. Servant, take
heed!

But before moving on to our other contribution to society—
light—I want us to think about some practical, positive aspects
of salt.

· **Salt is shaken and sprinkled . . . not poured.** It must be spread out. Too much salt *ruins* food. A good reminder for Christians to spread out rather than stay huddled all together.

· **Salt adds flavor . . . but it's obscure.** No one ever comments, "My, this is good salt." We frequently say, however, "The food is really tasty." Servants add zest to life, a flavor impossible to achieve without them.

· **Salt is unlike any other seasoning.** It's difference, however, is its strength. It can't be duplicated, and it must be applied before it is useful. Salt in the salt shaker does nobody any good! To help you develop this salt quality in your life, I heartily recommend a book by Rebecca Manley Pippert, *Out of the Saltshaker & Into the World,* an InterVarsity Press publication.[7] It is virtually impossible to read and apply her words and remain in the shaker!

The Light of the World

Does it seem important to you that Christ calls us what He called Himself?

> Again therefore Jesus spoke to them, saying, "I am the light of the world; he who follows Me shall not walk in the darkness, but shall have the light of life" (John 8:12).

Servants of Christ shine with His light in a society that is hopelessly lost, left to itself. Now, answer two questions:
1. What is the basic function of light?
2. How can that best occur?
The answer to the first question is obvious—to dispel darkness. Darkness cannot remain when a light is turned on. I don't care how thick the darkness may be. And the answer to the second question is found in Jesus' own words:

> You are the light of the world. A city set on a hill cannot be hidden.
> Nor do men light a lamp, and put it under the peck-measure,

but on the lampstand; and it gives light to all who are in the house (Matt. 5:14–16).

How can darkness be dispelled? First, by not hiding the light—*"set on a hill."* And second, by not limiting the light—*"on the lampstand . . . it gives light to all who are in the house.* What stars are to the night sky, servants are in a darkened world. It was this analogy that caused one writer to say:

> I sometimes think how splendid it would be if non-Christians, curious to discover the secret and source of our light, were to come up to us and enquire: "Twinkle, twinkle, little star, / How I wonder what you are!"[8]

We pose a weird phenomenon to those in darkness. They cannot figure us out! And that is exactly as Jesus planned it. Think of some distinctive characteristics of light:

· **Light is silent.** No noise, no big splash, no banners—light simply shines. It's like a single lighthouse along a rugged shoreline. All it does is shine as it turns.

· **Light gives direction.** No words, no sermon. Jesus says that others "see" our actions—but nothing is said of their hearing.

· **Light attracts attention.** You don't have to ask people to look at you when you turn a light on in a dark room. It happens automatically. If you are a Christian on an athletic team filled with non-Christians, you are the light in darkness. If you are a Christian family in a non-Christian neighborhood, you are the light in that darkness. The same is true if you are the only Christian nurse on your floor, or student in your school, or professional in your firm or group, or salesman in your district. You are a light in darkness—a servant of God who is being watched, who gives off a very distinct message . . . often with hardly a word being said. At first they may hate the light—but don't worry, they are still attracted to it. Let it shine! Don't attempt to show off how bright and sparkling you are, just shine! Dr. Martyn Lloyd-Jones emphasizes this:

As we produce and reveal it in our daily lives, we must remember that the Christian does not call attention to himself. Self has been forgotten in this poverty of spirit, in the meekness and all the other things. In other words, we are to do everything for God's sake, and for His glory. Self is to be absent, and must be utterly crushed in all its subtlety, for His sake, for His glory.

It follows from this that we are to do these things in such a way as to lead other men to glorify Him, and glory in Him, and give themselves to Him. "Let your light so shine before men, that they may see your good works." Yes; and so see them that they will themselves glorify your Father; you are to do so in order that these other people may glorify Him also.[9]

What a great reminder.

The "village" is in sad shape. Difficult, depraved, and deceived, those who live in it are living tasteless, hopeless lives. They need *salt* and they need *light* . . . the two ingredients a servant of God models.

Personal Response to Our Role

Since God has called us to be His salt-and-light servants in a bland, dark society, it will be necessary for us to commit ourselves to the task before us. Remember, salt must not lose its taste and light must not be hidden. In order to keep us on target, let me suggest three statements that declare and describe how to fulfill this role.

1. **"I am different."** Probably the greatest tragedy of Christianity through its changing and checkered history has been our tendency to become like the world rather than completely different from it. The prevailing culture has sucked us in like a huge vacuum cleaner, and we have done an amazing job of conforming.

But servants are to be different. As one man put it, "as different as chalk is from cheese." As different as salt is from decayed meat . . . as light is from the depths of Carlsbad Caverns. No veneer, remember. We are authentically different.

2. **"I am responsible."** If I read Jesus' words correctly, I see more than being salt and light. I am responsible for my salt not losing its bite and my light not becoming obscure or hidden. Every once in awhile it is helpful to ask some very hard questions of myself. True servants do more than *talk*. We refuse to become the "rabbit-hole Christians" John Stott speaks of, popping out of our holes and racing from our insulated caves to all-Christian gatherings only to rush back again. For salt to be tasted and for light to be seen, we must make contact. We are personally responsible.

3. **"I am influential."** Let's not kid ourselves. The very fact that we belong to Christ—that we don't adopt the system, that we march to a different drumbeat—gives us an influence in this society of ours. Maybe the quaint old "keeper of the springs" was not seen very much, but his role meant survival to that village in the Alps. We *are* influencing others—even when we aren't trying to act "religious" or preach from a soapbox.

I mentioned earlier a book by Rebecca Pippert. She tells a story in it that perfectly illustrates how we impact others without even trying. It is a classic example of the world's strange reaction to the presence of a Christian.

Sometimes non-Christians will act oddly around us because they are genuinely convicted by the Holy Spirit in us, and that's good. But all too often they are behaving "differently" because they feel that is the way they are supposed to act around religious types.

I am often put in a religious box when people discover what my profession is. Because I travel a great deal, I have a clergy card which sometimes enables me to travel at reduced rates. The only problem is that occasionally ticket agents won't believe I am authorized to use it! A young female just isn't what they have in mind when they see a clergy card. More than once I've been asked, "Okay, honey, now where did you rip this off?"

Once when I was flying from San Francisco to Portland I arrived at the counter and was greeted by an exceedingly friendly male ticket agent.

"Well, hel-lo-o-o there!" he said.

"Ah . . . I'd like to pick up my ticket to Portland, please."

"Gee, I'm sorry. You won't be able to fly there tonight."

"Why? Is the flight canceled?"

"No, it's because you're going out with me tonight."

"What?"

"Listen, I know this great restaurant with a hot band. You'll never regret it."

"Oh, I'm sorry, I really must get to Portland. Do you have my ticket?"

"Aw, what's the rush? I'll pick you up at eight. . . ."

"Look, I really must go to Portland," I said.

"Well, okay. Too bad though. Hey, I can't find your ticket." He paused, then said, "Looks like it's a date then!"

"Oh, I forgot to tell you, it's a . . . special ticket," I said.

"Oh, is it youth fare?"

"No, um, well, it's . . . ah, *clergy,*" I whispered, leaning over the counter.

He froze. "What did you say?"

"It's clergy."

"CLERGY!?!" he shouted, as the entire airport looked our way. His face went absolutely pale, as he was horrified by only one thought. "Oh, no. I flirted with a nun!"

When he disappeared behind the counter, I could hear him whisper to the other ticket agent a few feet away, "Hey, George, get a load of that girl up there. She's *clergy.*" Suddenly another man rose from behind the counter, smiled and nodded and disappeared again. I never felt so religious in my entire life.[10]

That's the price we pay, I suppose, for being authentic servants of the Master. Even when we aren't trying, out comes the salt and on comes the light!

10

The Perils of a Servant

Nobody in this generation will ever forget Jonestown. At least, I hope not: That tragedy stands as a mute reminder of the awful results of a leader gone wild.

I shall never be able to erase from my mind the scene that appeared on one television newscast after another. It was not just death, but a mass suicide—over nine hundred bloated corpses in the steamy jungle of Guyana. People in rows, "looking like full-grown rag dolls," was how one reporter described them. Except for a few defectors who managed to slip away at the last minute, every soul in that cult compound gave up his or her life as the leader demanded. Whoever takes the time to investigate the evidence that led to such a bizarre atrocity soon discovers that the man at the top (who claimed to be a servant of God) fell into the trap that has ruined many a strong, natural leader.

Beneath every horrible picture of that unforgettably sick scene could be written the same five-word caption: THE PERIL

OF LIMITLESS CONTROL. Rather than remaining a servant of God and of the people, instead of modeling humility, teachability, and unselfishness, Jim Jones eroded into an empty shell of authoritarianism, sensuality, and unaccountability . . . an untouchable prima donna who fell into the clutches of his own lust and pride.

Most every calling and occupation carries with it peculiar hazards—some subtle, some obvious and overt. It's not just the steeplejack or submarine crew or high-rise window washers or S.W.A.T. teams who face perils in their work. We all do. No exceptions.

Including servants.

That may surprise you. Being a servant seems as safe and harmless as a poached egg on a plate. What could possibly be perilous about serving others?

Some Common Misconceptions

As we return to a section of Scripture we looked at earlier, 2 Corinthians 4, I'd like to suggest three familiar misconceptions regarding servanthood. Read verses 4 through 7 rather carefully:

> . . . in whose case the god of this world has blinded the minds of the unbelieving, that they might not see the light of the gospel of the glory of Christ, who is the image of God.
>
> For we do not preach ourselves but Christ Jesus as Lord, and ourselves as your bond-servants for Jesus' sake.
>
> For God, who said, "Light shall shine out of darkness," is the One who has shone in our hearts to give the light of the knowledge of the glory of God in the face of Christ.
>
> But we have this treasure in earthen vessels, that the surpassing greatness of the power may be of God and not from ourselves.

Sounds like servants comprise an elite body of people, doesn't it? They possess a treasure. The "surpassing greatness" of God's power pours out of their lives. But when you look closely, you detect that all of that is of God, not themselves. This introduces misconception number one:

Servants Have Special Powers in Themselves

How very easy it is to look at God's servants through rose-colored glasses!—almost as if they possess a mystical, divine unction or some angelic "mantle" that causes them to ooze with supernatural, heaven-sent power. But this is wrong! Listen to an earlier verse:

Not that we are adequate in ourselves to consider anything as coming from ourselves, but our adequacy is from God (2 Cor. 3:5).

Mark it well, servants are absolutely human, filled with all the weaknesses and potential for failure that characterize every other human being.

Another common misconception is this:

Servants Don't Struggle with Everyday Problems

Consider 2 Corinthians 4:8–9:

. . . we are afflicted in every way, but not crushed; perplexed, but not despairing; persecuted, but not forsaken; struck down, but not destroyed.

Afflicted. Perplexed. Persecuted. Struck down. We'll look deeper into these terms in Chapter 12, but suffice it to say that they reflect the struggles common to all of us. Under stress, confused, pursued, rejected—Paul (and every servant since his day) understands what it means to endure the constant blast of problems. In fact, it is in the crucible that the servant learns to release his way for God's way.

Servants do indeed struggle with daily difficulties.

A third misconception:

Servants Are Protected against Subtle Dangers

Read verses 10–11:

> . . . always carrying about in the body the dying of Jesus, that the life of Jesus also may be manifested in our body.
> For we who live are constantly being delivered over to death for Jesus' sake, that the life of Jesus also may be manifested in our mortal flesh (2 Cor. 4:10–11).

People who serve God and others "carry about in the body" signs of death—dangers and perils that are undeniable. Subtle and silent, these dangers lurk in the most unexpected places, pleading for satisfaction. The true servant, as we have already discovered, is vulnerable. When the servant stumbles into these traps, it isn't long before he is completely ensnared. And it seldom happens fast or boldly. Usually, it comes on the scene in another garb entirely, appearing to be anything but dangerous.

Speaking of this, one man admits about the godly leader:

> Although he is by no means immune to the temptations of the flesh, the dangers most to be guarded against lie in the realm of the spirit. He must remember that "sabbathless Satan," his relentless enemy, will take advantage of every inch of ground he concedes in any area of his life.[1]

So let's not be misled. Servants, no matter how useful, godly, unselfish, and admirable, are every bit as human and subject to the perils of life as any other person on earth. Without special powers in themselves, as we have noted, they struggle with everyday problems . . . especially vulnerable to the subtle dangers that can easily trip them up, as we have already realized from the reminder of Jonestown.

A CLASSIC EXAMPLE

To illustrate the truth of this in Scripture, let's turn back to the Old Testament for a change and lift out of obscurity a man who became the helper of one of the greatest prophets God ever raised up. The prophet's name was *Elisha* and his servant's name was *Gehazi*. The story we want to examine starts in 2 Kings, chapter 2.

Background and Role

Times were hard. The nation of Israel was rapidly deteriorating as one wicked ruler following another led the people into increasing depths of depravity. The citizens became wasted, confused, empty shells of humanity. Morally, spiritually, politically, even physically their lives were *zilch!* The few prophets who did appear on the scene stood absolutely alone like cattle in a blizzard, but nevertheless, they *stood.*

Elijah (not to be confused with Elisha), a remarkably courageous prophet of God, had lived out his life by this time. As he departed "by a whirlwind to heaven" (2:1, 11), Elisha (his successor) is standing by and receives from God the same dynamic power that had rested on Elijah. With a whoosh, Elisha was off and running! God had a number of remarkable, even miraculous things for His prophet to do. And on top of all that, he soon comes to be known as a "man of God," a title he well deserved.

The prophet emerges in 2 Kings 4 with a servant named Gehazi. We pick up the story at verse 8:

> Now there came a day when Elisha passed over to Shunem, where there was a prominent woman, and she persuaded him to eat food. And so it was, as often as he passed by, he turned in there to eat food.
>
> And she said to her husband, "Behold now, I perceive that this is a holy man of God passing by us continually.
>
> "Please, let us make a little walled upper chamber and let us set a bed for him there, and a table and a chair and a lampstand; and it shall be, when he comes to us, that he can turn in there."
>
> One day he came there and turned in to the upper chamber and rested.
>
> Then he said to Gehazi his servant, "Call this Shunammite." And when he had called her, she stood before him.

And he said to him, "Say now to her, 'Behold, you have been careful for us with all this care; what can I do for you? Would you be spoken for to the king or to the captain of the army?'" And she answered, "I live among my own people."

So he said, "What then is to be done for her?" And Gehazi answered, "Truly she has no son and her husband is old."

And he said, "Call her." When he had called her, she stood in the doorway.

Then he said, "At this season next year you shall embrace a son." And she said, "No, my lord, O man of God, do not lie to your maidservant."

And the woman conceived and bore a son at that season the next year, as Elisha had said to her (vv. 8–17).

This is only the beginning of a series of events Elisha is involved in. But our attention falls upon the one whose job it was to assist the prophet. We want to discover through his experiences some of the common perils that await all who determine to serve others.

Temptations and Reactions

Working alongside a high-profile, greatly respected prophet like Elisha was a privilege. But at the same time it was a particular position that brought about unique temptations, as we shall see. We'll call these temptations, and Gehazi's reactions to them, "perils." I find four of them in Elisha's servant's life. The first is set forth in 2 Kings 4:18–26:

When the child was grown, the day came that he went out to his father to the reapers.

And he said to his father, "My head, my head." And he said to his servant, "Carry him to his mother."

When he had taken him and brought him to his mother, he sat on her lap until noon, and then died.

And she went up and laid him on the bed of the man of God, and shut the door behind him, and went out.

Then she called to her husband and said, "Please send me one of the servants and one of the donkeys, that I may run to the man of God and return."

And he said, "Why will you go to him today? It is neither new moon nor Sabbath." And she said, "It will be well."

Then she saddled a donkey and said to her servant, "Drive and go forward; do not slow down the pace for me unless I tell you."

So she went and came to the man of God to Mount Carmel. And it came about when the man of God saw her at a distance, that he said to Gehazi his servant, "Behold, yonder is the Shunammite.

"Please run now to meet her and say to her, 'Is it well with you? Is it well with your husband? Is it well with the child?'" And she answered, "It is well."

The "miracle child" God gave the Shunammite woman grows up and is old enough to work in the fields. While doing so he either receives a severe blow on his forehead or suffers a sunstroke or some serious internal problem, causing the young lad to cry out, "My head, my head!" Naturally, the mother thinks immediately of Elisha—if anybody can help, *he* can. When the prophet saw her coming at a distance, he recognized her. It is at this point we see the servant's tendency to react incorrectly. Read verses 26 through 28:

"Please run now to meet her and say to her, 'Is it well with you? Is it well with your husband? Is it well with the child?'" And she answered, "It is well."

When she came to the man of God to the hill, she caught hold of his feet. And Gehazi came near to push her away; but the man of God said, "Let her alone, for her soul is troubled within her; and the Lord has hid it from me and has not told me."

Then she said, "Did I ask for a son from my lord? Did I not say, 'Do not deceive me'?"

The Peril of Overprotection and Possessiveness

Do you see how this reveals itself? Gehazi is obviously committed to Elisha. He wants to be a protective shield around him—so we shouldn't be surprised that when the anxious mother arrived, Gehazi "came near to push her away." It's so easy for those with a servant's heart to get tunnel vision and miss the needs of others. A similar situation occurred in the account in Numbers 11:24–30 when Joshua attempted to restrain two men from prophesying in the camp. He was jealous that nobody took anything away from the special role of Moses, whom he served. Prophesying was Moses' job, not theirs! Greathearted Moses told Joshua to back off. Joshua attempted to overprotect Moses much like Gehazi did with Elisha.

Servants, watch out for the peril of possessiveness.

Let's read on through the 2 Kings 4 passage:

> Then he said to Gehazi, "Gird up your loins and take my staff in your hand, and go your way; if you meet any man, do not salute him, and if anyone salutes you, do not answer him; and lay my staff on the lad's face."
> And the mother of the lad said, "As the Lord lives and as you yourself live, I will not leave you." And he arose and followed her (vv. 29–30).

Elisha laid out a plan whereby the young man would be raised up . . . and that plan included Gehazi. The servant is dispatched to the bedside of the mother's son. We can be sure Gehazi's heart was beating fast. He must have anticipated an exciting response, as God would surely raise the lad from death. He would be involved in a miracle! But nothing happened. Not a thing changed.

> Then Gehazi passed on before them and laid the staff on the lad's face, but there was neither sound nor response. So he returned to meet him and told him, "The lad has not awakened" (v. 31).

Suddenly, Elisha burst on the scene—and phenomenal results occurred. A miracle transpired.

> When Elisha came into the house, behold the lad was dead and laid on his bed.
> So he entered and shut the door behind them both, and prayed to the Lord.

And he went up and lay on the child, and put his mouth on his mouth and his eyes on his eyes and his hands on his hands, and he stretched himself on him; and the flesh of the child became warm.

Then he returned and walked in the house once back and forth, and went up and stretched himself on him; and the lad sneezed seven times and the lad opened his eyes.

And he called Gehazi and said, "Call this Shunammite." So he called her. And when she came in to him, he said, "Take up your son."

Then she went in and fell at his feet and bowed herself to the ground, and she took up her son and went out.

Try to identify with the servant rather than with the ecstatic mother if you can. As you do so, you'll feel some of the very human feelings Gehazi must have had.

The Peril of Feeling Used and Unappreciated

Serve others long enough and you'll periodically dip into this valley. Gehazi had done exactly what he was told to do. Yet he had witnessed no change, no miracle. In came Elisha who suddenly did it all. And guess who is given the assignment to tell the mother—Gehazi! And if that isn't sufficient, read on—same song, second verse:

When Elisha returned to Gilgal, there was a famine in the land. As the sons of the prophets were sitting before him, he said to his servant, "Put on the large pot and boil stew for the sons of the prophet."

Then one went out into the field to gather herbs, and found a wild vine and gathered from it his lap full of wild gourds, and came and sliced them into the pot of stew, for they did not know what they were.

So they poured it out for the men to eat. And it came about as they were eating of the stew, that they cried out and said, "O man of God, there is death in the pot." And they were unable to eat (vv. 38–40).

Famine has struck the area. Our friend, Gehazi, is told to whip up a pot of stew. Inadvertently, poisonous plants are dropped into the crockpot and everybody screams! But then notice what happened:

> But he said, "Now bring meal." And he threw it into the pot, and he said, "Pour it out for the people that they may eat." Then there was no harm in the pot (v. 41).

Gehazi had done the work . . . but Elisha got all the credit. I mean, the servant can't even make stew! How frustrated can one get? Unless I miss my guess, a little embarrassment was added to the frustration . . . and Gehazi probably felt the sting of not being appreciated. You know, always being preempted by the prophet. Even though he had done everything he had been told to do.

So it is with servants today. It is so easy to feel used and unappreciated.

Do I write to you who serve behind the scenes in a ministry or a business? You work faithfully and diligently, yet the glory goes to another. Your efforts make someone else successful. How easy to feel resentful! Assistant directors, associate and assistant pastors, secretaries, administrators, "internal personnel," all members of the I-work-hard-but-because-I'm-not-up-front-I-never-get-the-credit club, *take heart!* Our God who rewards in secret will never overlook your commitment.

> For God is not unjust so as to forget your work and the love which you have shown toward His name, in having ministered and in still ministering to the saints (Heb. 6:10).

A great verse for those of you who feel used and unappreciated.

But a warning is also in order. Keep a close eye on your pride. God's true servant is like the Lord Jesus, who came not "to be served, but to serve, and to give His life a ransom for many" (Mark 10:45) . . . to serve and to give. Pride wants strokes—lots of them. It loves to get the credit, to be mentioned, to receive glory, to have people—ooh and ahhh. Ideally, your superiors will be thoughtful people who give you the credit you deserve, but, unfortunately, that will not always occur. And your pride will need to be held in check. At those tough times when you make the stew and someone else gets the strokes, remember your role: to serve and to give.

J. Oswald Sanders is correct when he writes this of pride:

> Nothing is more distasteful to God than self-conceit. This first and fundamental sin in essence aims at enthroning self at the expense of God. . . .
>
> Pride is a sin of whose presence its victim is least conscious. . . .
>
> If we are honest, when we measure ourselves by the life of our Lord who humbled Himself even to death on a cross, we cannot but be overwhelmed with the tawdriness and shabbiness, and even the vileness, of our hearts.[2]

True love flowing from authentic servants does not keep a record of who did what, and it does not look to others for the credit. In other words, real servants stay conscious of the blindness pride can create.

As we turn to chapter 5 in 2 Kings, an entirely different experience awaits Gehazi, the servant of Elisha. Not one but *two* more perils lurk in the shadows to ensnare the man. As we shall see, the second of the two proved too great a temptation for him and he finally succumbed. But first, let's set the stage.

A man named Naaman was a high-ranking Syrian soldier. He was influential, wealthy, proud, a man of dignity, courage, patriotism, and military clout. There was only one problem, the man had leprosy. Through a chain of interesting events, Naaman was led to Elisha for cleansing from his dread disease. We pick up the biblical narrative at verse 9:

> So Naaman came with his horses and his chariots, and stood at the doorway of the house of Elisha.
>
> And Elisha sent a messenger to him, saying, "Go and wash in the Jordan seven times, and your flesh shall be restored to you and you shall be clean."

But Naaman was furious and went away and said, "Behold, I thought, 'He will surely come out to me, and stand and call on the name of the Lord his God, and wave his hand over the place, and cure the leper.'

"Are not Abanah and Pharpar, the rivers of Damascus, better than all the waters of Israel? Could I not wash in them and be clean?" So he turned and went away in a rage.

I take it that the "messenger" Elisha sent to answer the door was Gehazi, his trusted servant. It fell his lot to be the bearer of news the Syrian officer did not want to hear. As we read in the account, the high-ranking soldier was offended. He became *enraged.* And look who was caught in the crossfire—the servant. The dear guy didn't generate the news, he just communicated it . . . and boom! This introduces us to another peril common to those who faithfully serve others.

The Peril of Disrespect and Resentment

Gehazi has neither rank nor authority, yet his responsibility puts him in a most unpopular dilemma. He has the task of facing a person with the truth that the person does not want to hear. The result? Feeling and hearing the verbal blows of disrespect and resentment. Let me stretch this out and apply it.

There are times when God's servant is called upon to confront or in some way tell another the truth that the individual does not want to hear. The information may be painful to accept, but it is what God wants said. So the faithful servant says it. Graciously yet accurately. And all of a sudden the lid blows sky high. He is caught in the crossfire. What do you do in such precarious moments? Fight back? Yell and scream and threaten in return?

Listen to God's counsel to servants whose job it is to say hard things:

And the Lord's bond-servant must not be quarrelsome, but be kind to all, able to teach, patient when wronged, with gentleness correcting those who are in opposition, if perhaps God may grant them repentance leading to the knowledge of the truth, and they may come to their senses and escape from the snare of the devil, having been held captive by him to do his will (2 Tim. 2:24–26).

What wise counsel! Not quarrelsome, but kind. Not irritated, but patient . . . even when wronged. Not angry, but gentle. God may be using your words to help the hearers "come to their senses," which may sound very noble; but, believe me, there are times it's not a lot to write home about.

As a pastor and a counselor, I frequently find myself in this unpopular spot. An individual who has come to me pours out his soul, not unlike the leper, Naaman. And God very clearly leads me to confront or point out a few specifics that the person finds rather painful to hear, not to mention accept. Suddenly, *I* become the verbal punching bag. Now understand, I didn't write the Book and I in no way view myself as the individual's judge—even though he may think I do. But I have had counselees scream at me, curse, stomp out of the room, and share with me a piece of their mind they couldn't afford to lose. Some wait until later and write me one of those flaming missiles that burn your eyes when you read them. And what did I do to deserve that treatment? I told the truth. I simply carried a message as tactfully and well-timed as possible, but it was rejected—at least for awhile. But the payoff comes later on when the person realizes the truth was told and I really had his good at heart.

Sometimes it falls the lot of an attorney or a medical doctor to be the bearer of such news. One of the best (and most hilarious) examples I ever heard along this line happened to a dentist, who stood his ground and refused to budge. My good friend, Dr. James Dobson, tells the story better than I could ever describe it:

> In the absence of parental leadership, some children become extremely obnoxious and defiant, especially in public places. Perhaps the best example was a ten-year-old boy named Robert, who was a patient of my good friend Dr. William Slonecker. Dr. Slonecker said his pediatric staff dreaded the days when Robert was scheduled for an office visit. He literally attacked the clinic,

grabbing instruments and files and telephones. His passive mother could do little more than shake her head in bewilderment.

During one physical examination, Dr. Slonecker observed severe cavities in Robert's teeth and knew that the boy must be referred to a local dentist. But who would be given the honor? A referral like Robert could mean the end of a professional friendship. Dr. Slonecker eventually decided to send him to an older dentist who reportedly understood children. The confrontation that followed now stands as one of the classic moments in the history of human conflict.

Robert arrived in the dental office, prepared for battle.

"Get in the chair, young man," said the doctor.

"No chance!" replied the boy.

"Son, I told you to climb onto the chair, and that's what I intend for you to do," said the dentist.

Robert stared at his opponent for a moment and then replied, "If you make me get in that chair, I will take off all my clothes."

The dentist calmly said, "Son, take 'em off."

The boy forthwith removed his shirt, undershirt, shoes and socks, and then looked up in defiance.

"All right, son," said the dentist. "Now get on the chair."

"You didn't hear me," sputtered Robert. "I said if you make me get on that chair, I will take off all my clothes."

"Son, take 'em off," replied the man.

Robert proceeded to remove his pants and shorts, finally standing totally naked before the dentist and his assistant.

"Now, son, get in the chair," said the doctor.

Robert did as he was told, and sat cooperatively through the entire procedure. When the cavities were drilled and filled, he was instructed to step down from the chair.

"Give me my clothes now," said the boy.

"I'm sorry," replied the dentist. "Tell your mother that we're going to keep your clothes tonight. She can pick them up tomorrow."

Can you comprehend the shock Robert's mother received when the door to the waiting room opened, and there stood her pink son, as naked as the day he was born? The room was filled with patients, but Robert and his mom walked past them and into the hall. They went down a public elevator and into the parking lot, ignoring the snickers of onlookers.

The next day, Robert's mother returned to retrieve his clothes, and asked to have a word with the dentist. However, she did not come to protest. These were her sentiments: "You don't know how much I appreciate what happened here yesterday. You see, Robert has been blackmailing me about his clothes for years. Whenever we are in a public place, such as a grocery store, he makes unreasonable demands of me. If I don't immediately buy him what he wants, he threatens to take off all his clothes. You are the first person who had called his bluff, doctor, and the impact on Robert has been incredible."[3]

I suppose the moral of the story is this: Being a servant may not be very pleasant, but when you do and say what is right—unpopular though it may be—good will come. Or better, in the words of Solomon:

> When a man's ways are pleasing to the Lord, He makes even his enemies to be at peace with him (Prov. 16:7).

Gehazi needed that verse to claim back when Naaman threw his fit. And do you know what later happened to Naaman? He finally did precisely what he was told to do, and he received the miraculous result he had been promised.

> So he went down and dipped himself seven times in the Jordan, according to the word of the man of God; and his flesh was restored like the flesh of a little child, and he was clean (2 Kings 5:14).

Tremendous!

Unlike many you and I may help, this man returned to thank Elisha and Gehazi. He was so overwhelmed he offered a sizable gift of gratitude. Elisha refused any tangible thank you.

> When he returned to the man of God with all his company, and came and stood before him, he said, "Behold now, I know that there is no God in all the earth, but in Israel; so please take a present from your servant now."

But he said, "As the Lord lives, before whom I stand, I will take nothing." And he urged him to take it, but he refused.

And Naaman said, "If not, please let your servant at least be given two mules' load of earth; for your servant will no more offer burnt offering nor will he sacrifice to other gods, but to the Lord.

"In this matter may the Lord pardon your servant: when my master goes into the house of Rimmon to worship there, and he leans on my hand and I bow myself in the house of Rimmon, when I bow myself in the house of Rimmon the Lord pardon your servant in this matter."

And he said to him, "Go in peace." So he departed from him some distance (vv. 15–19).

But that's not the end of the account. You'll notice Naaman offered Gehazi a gift as well. And the prophet had refused it. But deep within the heart of the servant crouched a silent beast of the soul, greed—not uncommon among some servants. Lest you think I am being too harsh, read on:

But Gehazi, the servant of Elisha the man of God, thought, "Behold, my master has spared this Naaman the Syrian, by not receiving from his hands what he brought. As the Lord lives, I will run after him and take something from him."

So Gehazi pursued Naaman. When Naaman saw one running after him, he came down from the chariot to meet him and said, "Is all well?"

And he said, "All is well. My master has sent me, saying, 'Behold, just now two young men of the sons of the prophets have come to me from the hill country of Ephraim. Please give them a talent of silver and two changes of clothes.'"

And Naaman said, "Be pleased to take two talents." And he urged him, and bound two talents of silver in two bags with two changes of clothes, and gave them to two of his servants; and they carried them before him.

When he came to the hill, he took them from their hand and deposited them in the house, and he sent the men away, and they departed (2 Kings 5:20–24).

Got the picture? You have just read of the fourth and perhaps the most subtle peril every servant must endure: hidden greed.

The Peril of Hidden Greed

This is the secret, smoldering desire to be rewarded, applauded, and exalted. Elisha said, "No." No way did he want the soldier ever to say, "He did it for what he would get out of it," which prompted the prophet to respond as he did—"I will take nothing" (v. 16). But Gehazi was cut from another piece of cloth. Maybe he was weary of feeling used and unappreciated or perhaps he had had enough of just getting by on a shoestring. Whatever, he possessed some pretty strong feelings, since he second-guessed Elisha's decision (v. 20), falsified the story when he met up with Naaman (v. 22), and attempted to cover his tracks when he later stood before his master (v. 25). Listen to the tragic ending.

> But he went in and stood before his master. And Elisha said to him, "Where have you been, Gehazi?" And he said, "Your servant went nowhere."
> Then he said to him, "Did not my heart go with you, when the man turned from his chariot to meet you? Is it a time to receive money and to receive clothes and oliveyards and vineyards and sheep and oxen and male and female servants?
> "Therefore, the leprosy of Naaman shall cleave to you and to your descendants forever." So he went out from his presence a leper as white as snow (vv. 25–27).

Exposed and sternly judged, Gehazi experienced a horrible punishment. He had not only gone against the decision of the prophet, he had lied to him when confronted with his deeds. The servant was accountable! I repeat this same theme you have already read several times in this book. Accountability is essential in order for any servant to remain pure and pliable clay in the Master's hand. Would to God Jim Jones had applied that same truth before he began his downward spiral, taking hundreds with him.

Jim Jones is so unlike the man Rudyard Kipling had in mind when he wrote *If*. This poem is an undying challenge to every one of us who desires to serve:

If you can keep your head when all about you
Are losing theirs and blaming it on you;
If you can trust yourself when all men doubt you,
But make allowance for their doubting too;
If you can wait and not be tired by waiting,
Or being lied about, don't deal in lies,
Or being hated, don't give way to hating,
And yet don't look too good, nor talk too wise:

If you can dream—and not make dreams your
master;
If you can think—and not make thoughts your
aim;
If you can meet with Triumph and Disaster
And treat those two imposters just the same;

. . . .

If you can talk with crowds and keep your virtue,
Or walk with kings—nor lose the common
touch;
If neither foes nor loving friends can hurt you;
If all men count with you, but none too much;
If you can fill the unforgiving minute
With sixty seconds' worth of distance run—
Yours is the Earth and everything that's in it,
And—what is more—you'll be a Man, my son!

SOME LINGERING LESSONS

We have attempted to maintain an objective stance as we
have investigated the life of a servant in the Old Testament. We
have discovered four common perils he faced, identical to those
we wrestle with:
- Being overprotective and possessive of the one he served.
- Feeling used and unappreciated.
- Experiencing undeserved disrespect and resentment.
- Having hidden greed—desiring to be rewarded.

From these very real and common perils there emerges at least three timely lessons for all of us to remember.

1. **No servant is completely safe.** A tough truth to accept! We who give and give become increasingly more vulnerable as time passes. As I shall point out in my chapter on the consequences of serving others, there are times we'll get ripped off. We *will* be used. We *will* feel unappreciated. But realizing ahead of time this will happen, we are better equipped to handle it when it comes. The proper perspective will guard us against stumbling into one of these perils.

A statement from one of C. S. Lewis's books often comes to mind:

> To love at all is to be vulnerable. Love anything, and your heart will certainly be wrung and possibly be broken. If you want to make sure of keeping it intact, you must give your heart to no one, not even to an animal. Wrap it carefully round with hobbies and little luxuries; avoid all entanglements; lock it up safe in the casket or coffin of your selfishness. But in that casket—safe, dark, motionless, airless—it will change. It will not be broken; it will become unbreakable, impenetrable, irredeemable. . . . The only place outside Heaven where you can be perfectly safe from all the dangers . . . of love is Hell.[4]

No servant is completely safe. Lean hard on the Master when you serve others.

2. **Most deeds will be initially unrewarded.** Again, this is helpful to know before we plunge in head first. If you are the type who needs a lot of strokes from people, who has to be appreciated before you can continue very long, you'd better forget about being a servant. More often than not, you will be overlooked, passed up, behind the scenes, and virtually unknown. Your reward will not come from without, but from within. Not from people, but from the satisfaction God gives you down inside.

Much of the ministry requires this mentality. A pastor may stand at the door of the church following his sermon and shake hands with the flock as everybody says nice things about him (my friend Howard Hendricks calls this "the glorification of the worm," a description I certainly agree with), but in reality, if that man preaches for those few moments of flattery—*and most don't*—he's in the wrong business. True servants readily accept the truth of this familiar piece:

> So send I you to labor unrewarded.
> To serve unpaid, unloved, unsought, unknown,
> To bear rebuke, to suffer scorn and scoffing,
> So send I you to toil for Me alone. . . .
>
> So send I you to leave your life's ambition,
> To die to dear desire, self-will resign,
> To labor long and love where men revile you,
> So send I you to lose your life in Mine.
>
> "As the Father hath sent me, So send I you."[5]

Most of the servant's deeds will be initially unrewarded. That's a basic axiom we must accept.

3. **All motives must be honestly searched.** Learn a lesson from Gehazi. Before jumping, think to ask why. Before accepting any of Naaman's tangible gifts of gratitude (and there are occasions when such is perfectly acceptable), probe into your reason for doing so. Check your motive, fellow servant.

During my days in seminary, I formed a habit that helped me immensely throughout life. I had my artistic sister Luci print a simple, three-word question on a small rectangular card I placed on the wall above the desk where I spent so much of my time. Just black letters on a white card, with a bold question mark at the end:

What's Your Motive?

I no longer have the card, but the question is now indelibly etched on my mind. I ask it almost every day of my life. It has proven to be an essential checkpoint I now apply on a regular basis:

"Why are you planning this?"

"What's the reason behind your doing that?"

"Why did you say yes (or no)?"

"What is the motive for writing that letter?"

"Why are you excited over this opportunity?"

"What causes you to bring up that subject?"

"Why did you mention his/her name?"

"What's your motive, Swindoll?"

Searching, probing, penetrating questions. If Gehazi had only done that, the man would never have died as tragic a death as he did. Frankly, I'm grateful such extreme consequences don't happen to us today when our motives are wrong. If they did, churches would be full of people with leprosy.

Because the path of servanthood is so perilous, we need to cultivate a sensitive walk with God marked by *obedience*. This is so important, I have decided to dedicate the next chapter to it.

11

The Obedience of a Servant

A familiar essay anonymously written many years ago says this about Jesus Christ:

> Nineteen long centuries have come and gone and today he is the centerpiece of the human race and the leader of the column of progress. I am far within the mark when I say that all the armies that ever marched, all the navies that ever were built; all the parliaments that ever sat and all the kings that ever reigned, put together, have not affected the life of man upon this earth as powerfully as has that one solitary life.

The late Wilbur Smith, respected Bible scholar of the last generation, wrote:

> The latest edition of the *Encyclopaedia Britannica* gives twenty thousand words to this person, Jesus, and does not even hint that He did not exist—more words, by the way, than are given to Aristotle, Alexander, Cicero, Julius Caesar, or Napoleon Bonaparte.[1]

George Buttrick, in a *Life* magazine article, adds:

> Jesus gave history a new beginning. In every land he is at
> home. . . . His birthday is kept across the world. His death-day
> has set a gallows against every city skyline.[2]

Even Napoleon admitted:

> I know men and I tell you that Jesus Christ was no mere man:
> Between Him and whoever else in the world there is no possible
> term of comparison.[3]

Impressive words.

So goes the testimony of influential people—and they could
be multiplied by the hundreds—regarding the most phenomenal
Person who ever cast a shadow across earth's landscape.
Without question, He is unique. He is awesome in the truest
sense of the term.

But what was He like *personally* down inside His skin? Is there
any place, for example, where He describes *Himself?* The answer
is yes. Does that description fit the common idea of human
greatness? The answer is no. Unlike most influential, celebrity
types, Jesus' description of Himself doesn't sound like the
popular hype we've grown accustomed to hearing.

For example, recently I received in my daily stack of mail a
multicolored brochure advertising and announcing a series of
lectures to be delivered in Los Angeles by a man (a Christian
"superstar") who has traveled widely, whose name is familiar to
most folks in the family of God. I must confess I lifted my
eyebrows with surprise when I read these words written in that
brochure describing the man:

A phenomenal individual . . .
   In great demand around the world . . .
      Today's most sought-after speaker!

That's a far cry from the way Jesus Christ described Himself.

A SELF-DESCRIPTION OF JESUS

I've been involved in a serious study of Scripture for well over twenty years, and in all that time I have found only one place where Jesus Christ—in His own words—describes his own "inner man." In doing so, He uses only two words. Unlike the Los Angeles celebrity, those words are not *phenomenal* and *great.* He doesn't even mention that He was *sought after* as a speaker. Although it is true, He doesn't say: "I am wise and powerful," or "I am holy and eternal," or "I am all-knowing and absolute deity." Do you know what He said? Hold on, it may surprise you.

Come to Me, all who are weary and heavy-laden, and I will give you rest.
Take My yoke upon you, and learn from Me, for I am gentle and humble in heart; and YOU SHALL FIND REST FOR YOUR SOULS (Matt. 11:28–29).

I am *gentle.* I am *humble.* These are servant terms. *Gentle* is the same word we examined rather carefully in chapter 7 when we analyzed that particular characteristic of a servant. The word means strength under control. You may recall, it is used of a wild stallion that has been tamed. "Humble in heart" means lowly—the word picture of a helper. Unselfishness and thoughtfulness are in the description. It doesn't mean weak and insignificant, however.

Frankly, I find it extremely significant that when Jesus lifts the veil of silence and once for all gives us a glimpse of Himself, the real stuff of His inner person, He uses *gentle* and *humble.* As we came to realize early in this book, when we read that God the Father is committed to forming us to the image of His Son, qualities such as these are what He wants to see emerge. We are never more like Christ than when we fit into His description of Himself.

And how do those things reveal themselves? In what way do we reveal them the best? In our *obedience.* Servanthood and obedience go together like Siamese twins. And the finest illustration of this is the Son Himself who openly confessed, ". . . I do nothing on My own initiative . . . I always do the things that are pleasing to Him . . . (John 8:28–29). In other words, Jesus' self-description was verified by His obedience. Like no one else who has ever lived, He practiced what He preached.

ILLUSTRATION OF JESUS' SELF-DESCRIPTION

The gentle and humble lifestyle of the Savior is nowhere more evident than in the account of John 13 where He washed the feet of His friends, the disciples. In that event, He left us some timeless principles regarding servanthood we dare not ignore. If we are serious about "improving our serve," we must take time to learn and apply the facts as well as the implications of John 13:4–17.

Background Information

The scene before us in this chapter occurred in first-century Jerusalem. Paved roads were few. In fact, within most cities they were unheard of. The roads and alleys in Jerusalem were more like winding dirt trails, all covered with a thick layer of dust. When the rains came, those paths were liquid slush, several inches of thick mud. It was the custom, therefore, for the host to provide a slave at the door of his home to wash the feet of the dinner guests as they arrived. The servant knelt with a pitcher of water, a pan, and a towel and washed the dirt or mud off the feet as each guest prepared to enter the home. Shoes, boots, and sandals were left at the door, a custom still prevalent in the Far East. If a home could not afford a slave, one of the early arriving guests would graciously take upon himself the role of the house servant and wash the feet of those who came. What is interesting is that *none* of the disciples had volunteered for that lowly task . . . so the room was filled with proud hearts and dirty feet. Interestingly, those disciples were willing to fight for a throne, but not a towel. Things haven't changed a lot since then, by the way.

Personal Demonstration

Read rather carefully the account of what transpired:

> Jesus . . . rose from supper . . . and taking a towel, girded Himself about.
> Then He poured water into the basin, and began to wash the disciples' feet, and to wipe them with the towel with which He was girded.
> And so He came to Simon Peter. He said to Him, "Lord, do You wash my feet?"
> Jesus answered and said to him, "What I do you do not realize now; but you shall understand hereafter."
> Peter said to Him, "Never shall You wash my feet!" Jesus answered him, "If I do not wash you, you have no part with Me."
> Simon Peter said to Him, "Lord, not my feet only, but also my hands and my head."
> Jesus said to him, "He who has bathed needs only to wash his feet, but is completely clean; and you are clean, but not all of you."
> For He knew the one who was betraying Him; for this reason He said, "Not all of you are clean" (John 13:3–11).

As I meditate on the scene John describes for us, a couple or three observations about serving others emerge.

Being a Servant Is Unannounced

Jesus never said, "Men, I am now going to demonstrate servanthood—watch my humility." No way. That kind of obvious pride was the trademark of the Pharisees. If you wondered whether they were humble, all you had to do was hang around them awhile. Sooner or later they would announce it . . . which explains why Jesus came down so hard on them in Matthew 23.

Unlike those pious frauds, the Messiah slipped away from the table, quietly pulled off His outer tunic, and with towel, pitcher, and pan in hand, He moved quietly from man to man. Now understand, please, that they weren't sitting as they are portrayed in Leonardo da Vinci's work *The Last Supper*. All due respect for that genius, but he missed it when he portrayed the biblical scene through Renaissance eyes. They were not sitting in ladderback, dining-room chairs all on one side of a long table! In those days, people reclined at a meal, actually leaning on one elbow as they lay on their side on a small thin pad or a larger rug covering the floor. The table was a low, rectangular block of wood upon which the food was placed. And they ate with their hands, not utensils. This position meant that if your feet were not clean, your neighbor was very much aware of it. It would be hard to ignore a face full of dirty feet.

As Jesus reached Peter, I am sure most of the small talk had dwindled. By now, the men realized their wrong. Guilt had begun to push its way into their hearts. Peter must have drawn his feet up close to him when he said, in effect, "No! Not *my* feet. Never, ever, ever will you wash my feet, from now 'til eternity!" This reveals a second observation about having a gentle and humble heart.

Being a Servant Includes Receiving Graciously
as Well as Giving Graciously

Peter wasn't about to be that vulnerable. After all, Jesus was the Master. No way was He going to wash the dirt off Peter's feet! I ask you, is that humility? You know it's not. Being willing to *receive* sometimes takes more grace than giving to others. And our reluctance to do so really exposes our pride, doesn't it?

James "Frog" Sullivan, constantly on the move, heavily involved in one Christian meeting after another (with little regard for his own family's needs), faced a situation not unlike the one Peter experienced. His wife Carolyn broke emotionally. Frog had to admit her into a local psychiatric hospital for an extended period of time. With a mixture of intense feelings ranging from strong resentment and anger to confusion and guilt, he drove home a broken man and sat down to explain everything to their children, Cathy and Scott, that dark night. For the first time in their presence, this hard-charging, always-on-top, fast-moving leader and father began to cry. Listen to his honest admission:

Not knowing how long it was going to be, or whether she was ever going to come out cured, I took the children for a hamburger and talked with them endlessly. I got them ready for bed and continued to talk. I knew that night that I was facing a crisis in my own life that would either make me or ruin me. That afternoon I had gone to a friend's house and had taken a fifth of whiskey of theirs home with me. After I put those kids to bed and prayed with them, my little Cathy saw me cry for the first time in her life. She said: "Dad, I've never seen you cry before." I think that night she learned some things about her dad. That I was a man, that I was human, that I was hurt, alone and lonely.

I bathed, put on some pajamas, and headed for the icebox to mix a drink. At that very moment I think I acknowledged I was through with God for good, through with the Christian life I'd known because I had given everything to him and had now ended up with nothing but a hurt, lonely, confused wife and nest of problems. I was really angry, knowing once again that I had hurt Carolyn deeply. As I went to the refrigerator, the doorbell rang, and an unbelievably wonderful man, Jack Johnston, was standing in the doorway.

I had already prayed earlier that night, and in the middle of my prayer I told God that I didn't understand. I had kept my end of the bargain, but he had done this dastardly thing to me. I didn't even know where he was or what he wanted from me any longer. I had given him my life blood and my family, and now he was trying to destroy me. As Jack walked into the room, he grabbed me and hugged me tight for maybe ten or fifteen minutes, I don't remember. He hugged me so tight and with such strength of caring, that my anger, bitterness, and disappointment seemed transferred from my fragile soul to his very being. He never quoted verses, he never said everything was going to be all right; he just blessed me with a short prayer and walked out the door, carrying my hostilities into the night.

I didn't understand it then, and I don't pretend to understand it now. I still don't understand what happened to Carolyn. But because of Jack, I was able to accept the situation. The love we received from Christians in the next few months was astounding, overwhelmingly beautiful. Meals were brought into our home for one solid month. People came to make up our beds, clean our house. I received money in envelopes through the mail from unknown sources to help with medical expenses that soared out of sight . . .

The thing that destroys a good many of us as Christians is our inability to relate to each other in a warm, honest, compassionate sort of way. Even with those to whom I was close, I failed in this endeavor. I was so busy being a "doing" Christian (Boy, that certainly was me!) that I'd forgotten what God called me to be. For so long I didn't know that a Christian was supposed to let someone love him; I thought that he was always supposed to be loving somebody else. I didn't think it was necessary to let anyone love me, including Carolyn. It seems that in the context of my Christian faith, you were adequate if you could love people; but you were considered inadequate if you let them love you.[4]

I cannot criticize the man. I find those same self-sufficient tendencies in myself, I must confess. Being a super high-achiever, I find it difficult to receive from others. *Really* difficult. I'm usually on the giving end, not the receiving. My pride fights hard to stay intact.

This was brought home to me rather forcefully one Christmas season several years ago. A man in our church congregation drove over to our home with his Christmas gift to our family. Not something wrapped up in bright paper with a big ribbon, but a thoughtful gift of love demonstrated by washing all the windows of our home. I was studying that Saturday morning at my office at the church as my wife and our children welcomed him in. He quietly began doing the job. I drove up later that morning and immediately noticed his car out front. I wondered if there was perhaps some need (there I was again, thinking like I usually do).

The kids met me at the door with the news that Phil (not his real name) was there and was washing our windows. My immediate response, of course, was surprise. I knew he was a busy husband and father with many more things to do than clean my windows. I went to the patio and saw his smiling face.

"Phil, what's going on? Man, I can't believe this."

Still smiling, he responded, "Chuck, I just wanted to do this for you and your family. Merry Christmas!"

"Hey, Phil," (I'm now a little embarrassed) "what do you say you just finish up the patio doors, and we'll get the rest, okay?"

"Nope. I'd like to go all the way around."

"Gee, thanks, man . . . but you've got lots of other things more important to do. Tell you what, you get all the downstairs, and the kids and I will get the upstairs."

"No, I'd really like to get up there too."

"Well, uh—why don't you get the outside all the way around, and we'll get the inside?"

Phil paused, looked directly at me and said, "Chuck! I want to wash all the windows, upstairs and downstairs, inside and outside—every one of them. You are always giving. For a change, I'd like you to *receive.*"

Suddenly, I realized what a battle I have graciously receiving others' gifts. I understand Peter's reluctance. Servanthood was hard for him, especially when it called for receiving from someone else.

Jesus said a strong thing to Peter when He spoke these words: ". . . If I do not wash you, you have no part with me" (John 13:8). Our Lord's rebuke introduces a third observation.

Being a Servant Is Not a Sign of Inner Weakness, but Incredible Strength

There is no way to remove the jab and the twist from Christ's words to Peter. He said, in effect, "If you do not allow Me to do this, that is it. Get out!" Anybody who lives under the delusion that Christ was rather weak and spineless has overlooked such statements as this one. Being a servant in no way implies there will never be a confrontation or strong words shared with others. The Lord may choose to use the reproof of a servant who has earned the right to be heard even more often than that of an aggressive leader type.

It certainly worked with Peter. We know he got the message when he blurted out, in so many words, "Give me a bath!" No, that wasn't necessary, only his feet.

After Jesus brought back into balance Peter's overreaction, He sat down for a time of reflection and instruction among the men. John tells us what followed:

> And so when He had washed their feet, and taken His garments, and reclined at table again, He said to them, "Do you know what I have done to you?"

What a strange question. Obviously, they knew what He had done. He had washed their feet! But He had much more in mind than the obvious—Jesus always does. He wanted them to think deeply, to learn something very insightful and valuable as an obedient servant. Look at what He told them.

> "You call Me Teacher, and Lord; and you are right; for so I am.
> "If I then, the Lord and the Teacher, washed your feet, you also ought to wash one another's feet.
> "For I gave you an example that you also should do as I did to you.
> "Truly, truly, I say to you, a slave is not greater than his master; neither one who is sent greater than the one who sent him.
> "If you know these things, you are blessed if you do them" (John 13:13–17).

Direct Admonition

He threw them a curve. He began by stating His role of authority among them: the "Teacher," the "Lord." Now what would you expect they thought He would say next? The obvious: "I washed your feet—so—now you should wash My feet." I believe that's what they expected to hear, like our I-scratched-your-back-now-you-scratch-mine reaction.

But with Jesus, that would have been a privilege. Who *wouldn't* want to do that? We'd stand in line to wash our Savior's feet. But that is not what He said. That would not be anything near the epitome of servanthood.

He told them (and us) to wash *one another's* feet. What an admonition! "As I have done to you, you do to one another." Our obedience is put to the maximum test at that level.

Now here's the clincher, verse 15: "For I gave you an example that you also should do as I did to you."

Let's read it in a much more popular way:

"I gave you an example that you should study about it on Sundays." No.

Or . . .

"I gave you an example that you should form discussion groups and meditate on it." No.

Or how about . . .

"I gave you an example that you should memorize My words and repeat them often." No.

Jesus said it plainly. He was looking for action, not theory.

"I gave you an example that you should *do* as I did to you."

To make the value of obedience just as practical as possible, let's play "Let's pretend." Let's pretend that you work for me. In fact, you are my executive assistant in a company that is growing rapidly. I'm the owner and I'm interested in expanding overseas. To pull this off, I make plans to travel abroad and stay there until the new branch office gets established. I make all the arrangements to take my family in the move to Europe for six to eight months, and I leave you in charge of the busy stateside organization. I tell you that I will write you regularly and give you direction and instructions.

I leave and you stay. Months pass. A flow of letters are mailed from Europe and received by you at the national headquarters. I spell out all my expectations. Finally, I return. Soon after my arrival I drive down to the office. I am stunned! Grass and weeds have grown up high. A few windows along the street are broken. I walk into the receptionist's room and she is doing her nails, chewing gum, and listening to her favorite disco station. I look around and notice the waste baskets are overflowing, the carpet hasn't been vacuumed for weeks, and nobody seems concerned that the owner has returned. I ask about your whereabouts and someone in the crowded lounge area points down the hall and yells, "I think he's down there." Disturbed, I move in that direction and bump into you as you are finishing a chess game with our sales manager. I ask you to step into my office (which has been temporarily turned into a television room for watching afternoon soap operas).

"What in the world is going on, man?"

"What do ya' mean, Chuck?"

"Well, look at this place! Didn't you get any of my letters?"

"Letters? Oh, yeah—sure, got every one of them. As a matter of fact, Chuck, we have had *letter study* every Friday night since you left. We have even divided all the personnel into small groups and discussed many of the things you wrote. Some of those things were really interesting. You'll be pleased to know that a few of us have actually committed to memory some of your sentences and paragraphs. One or two memorized an entire letter or two! Great stuff in those letters!"

"Okay, okay—you got my letters, you studied them and meditated on them, discussed and even memorized them. *BUT WHAT DID YOU DO ABOUT THEM?*"

"Do? Uh—we didn't *do* anything about them."

Sound a little familiar?

Jesus, the Lord, goes to the bottom line here in John 13. "I left you an example of what you should *do*—carry out my directions, fulfill my commands, follow my instructions." That's obedience—doing what we are told to do. He washed dirty feet, then He said, "You do that too." Meaning that we are to serve others. Let's understand, however, that the right attitude must accompany the right actions. Be careful with the temperature of the water you use! It's easy to use boiling water when you "wash feet" . . . or ice cold water. I know some who have come pretty close to dry cleaning a few feet. Ah, that's bad. The goal is to remove dirt, not skin, from the feet.

Appropriation of Christ's Instruction

As we think about these things and attempt to read them as our Savior meant them, we realize the tremendous emphasis He put on obedience. As we have seen before, this was a major difference between Him and the Pharisees. They loved to dwell in the realm of theory. Hypocrisy marked their steps. They talked a good fight when it came to servanthood . . . but they lacked the one ingredient that could make everything authentic: *obedience*. Perhaps that explains why He came down so strong on it.

As I think about appropriating Christ's model and command, three specifics seem important enough to mention.

1. Obedience means personal involvement.

If I then, the Lord and the Teacher, washed your feet, you also ought to wash one another's feet (John 13:14).

We cannot serve one another in absentia or at arm's length. It means if someone is drowning in a troubled sea, we get wet, we get in touch. It means if someone drifts away, we don't ignore that person, we reach out to help and restore. Nobody ever learned how to water ski in the living room through a correspondence course. You have to get into the water and get personally involved. Think about this. Honestly now, are you willing to get involved and help at least one person in need? Willingness must precede involvement.

2. Obedience requires Christlike unselfishness.

For I gave you an example that you also should do as I did to you (John 13:15).

Let your eyes dig into those words. To pull off this concept, we'll need to see others as Christ sees them. We'll need to risk reaching out, giving up the luxury of staying safe . . . giving up *our* preferences for His. Unselfishness never comes easy.

3. Obedience results in ultimate happiness.

If you know these things, you are blessed if you do them (John 13:17).

Notice, in the final analysis happiness comes from *doing* these things. Meaning what? Namely this, we have to carry it out before we can enter into the joy of serving. Just studying about it or discussing it produces no lasting happiness. The fun comes when we roll up our sleeves, wrap the towel around our waist, and wash a few feet . . . quietly . . . graciously . . . cheerfully . . . like Christ who was "gentle" and "humble in heart."

Does that mean it will never backfire on us? Am I saying those with servant hearts will not get ripped off or hurt in the process? Does this promise of happiness mean we'll be protected from suffering? No, *a thousand times no!* To keep everything realistic, we must face the very painful consequences. Even when we have been "gentle" and "humble in heart." What else can we expect? The perfect Model of obedience finished His earthly life as a corpse on a cross.

The next chapter will help keep all of this in proper perspective. There are often consequences connected with serving, even when we have been obedient. And those consequences are neither pleasant nor expected, as we shall see. Brace yourself, fellow servant. This may hurt a little.

12

The Consequences of Serving

We Americans like things to be logical and fair. We not only like that, we operate our lives on that basis. Logic and fairness are big guns in our society.

Meaning this: If I do what is right, good will come to me, and if I do what is wrong, bad things will happen to me. Right brings rewards and wrong brings consequences. That's a very logical and fair axiom of life, but there's only one problem with it. *It isn't always true.* Life doesn't work out quite that well. There isn't a person reading these words who hasn't had the tables turned. All of us have had the unhappy and unfortunate experience of doing what is right, yet we suffered for it. And we have also done what is wrong on a few occasions without being punished. The latter, we can handle rather easily . . . but the former is a tough pill to swallow.

I don't find it a nagging problem, for example, to drive 65 miles an hour on the highway and get away with it. Normally, I don't lie awake through the night feeling bad because an officer failed to give me a ticket—even though, in all fairness, I deserved one. But you let one of those guys ticket me when I have done nothing wrong, and I'm fit to be tied! And so are you. We *hate* being ripped off. Consequences belong to wrong actions. When they attach themselves to right actions, we struggle with resentment and anger.

A REALISTIC APPRAISAL OF SERVING

I wish I could say that the only place such things happen is in our driving, but I cannot. They also happen in our serving. You will give, forgive, forget, release your own will, obey God to the maximum, and wash dirty feet with an attitude of gentleness and humility. And after all those beautiful things, you will get ripped off occasionally. I want all of us to enter into this ministry of servanthood with our eyes wide open. If we serve others long enough, we will suffer wrong treatment for doing right things. Knowing all this ahead of time will help "improve your serve," believe me.

Suffering for Doing What Is Right

The Bible doesn't hide this painful reality from us. In 1 Peter 2:20-24 (addressed to servants, by the way—see verse 18), we read:

> For what credit is there if, when you sin and are harshly treated, you endure it with patience? But if when you do what is right and suffer for it you patiently endure it, this finds favor with God.
>
> For you have been called for this purpose, since Christ also suffered for you, leaving you an example for you to follow in His steps, WHO COMMITTED NO SIN, NOR WAS ANY DECEIT FOUND IN HIS MOUTH; and while being reviled, He did not revile in return; while suffering, He uttered no threats, but kept entrusting Himself to Him who judges righteously; and He Himself bore our sins in His body on the cross, that we might die to sin and live to righteousness; for by His wounds you were healed.

Part of this "makes sense," according to our logical and fair standard. Part of it doesn't. If a person does wrong and then suffers the consequences, even though he or she patiently endures the punishment, nobody applauds. Who is really impressed, for example, if Charles Manson quietly spends his years behind bars without complaining? It's no great virtue.

But—now get this clearly fixed in your mind—when you do what is *right* and suffer for it with grace and patience, God applauds! Illustration: Jesus Christ's suffering and death on the cross. He, the perfect God-man, was mistreated, hated, maligned, beaten, and finally nailed to a cruel cross. He suffered awful consequences even though He spent His life giving and serving. Listen to 1 Peter 3:17–18:

> For it is better, if God should will it so, that you suffer for doing what is right rather than for doing what is wrong.
> For Christ also died for sins once for all, the just for the unjust, in order that He might bring us to God, having been put to death in the flesh, but made alive in the spirit.

One thing is certain: If people treated a perfect individual that way, then imperfect people cannot expect to escape mistreatment. If it hasn't happened to you yet, it will. In light of that fact, I would like to dedicate this chapter to those of you who have been mistreated in the past, and to those who are now being mistreated . . . as well as to those who will be mistreated in the future!

Responding to Treatment that Is Wrong

The consequence of serving is no new phenomenon. It goes a long way back in time. Greathearted, loving, caring, sacrificial servants of the living God have known ill-treatment down through the centuries. I'm not aware of a more moving section of Scripture than these verses out of Hebrews 11, which declare the reality of the consequences of serving:

And some women, through faith, received their loved ones back again from death. But others trusted God and were beaten to death, preferring to die rather than turn from God and be free— trusting that they would rise to a better life afterwards.

Some were laughed at and their backs cut open with whips, and others were chained in dungeons. Some died by stoning and some by being sawed in two; others were promised freedom if they would renounce their faith, then were killed with the sword. Some went about in skins of sheep and goats, wandering over deserts and mountains, hiding in dens and caves. They were hungry and sick and ill-treated—too good for this world. And these men of faith, though they trusted God and won his approval, none of them received all that God had promised them (Heb. 11:35–39, TLB).

Tortured. Rejected. Threatened. Hungry. Sick. Martyred. People who were "too good for this world" were kicked around like big rag dolls . . . even though they gave and they served. If it happened to them—need I say more? Yes, maybe I should.

My major goal in this chapter is to help prepare you for the inevitable. Bitterness is often bred in a context of disillusionment. Many a Christian, unfortunately, is sidelined today, eaten up by the acid of resentment and bitterness, because he or she was mistreated after doing what was right. If this chapter will preserve you from the paralyzing sting of bitterness and disillusionment, it will have served its purpose.

THE DARK SIDE OF SERVING

Let's go back to 2 Corinthians, chapter 4, a section of Scripture we've looked at several times already. Perhaps, then, you remember these words:

For we do not preach ourselves but Christ Jesus as Lord, and ourselves as your bond-servants for Jesus' sake.

For God, who said, "Light shall shine out of darkness," is the

One who has shone in our hearts to give the light of the knowledge of the glory of God in the face of Christ.

But we have this treasure in earthen vessels, that the surpassing greatness of the power may be of God and not from ourselves (2 Cor. 4:5–7).

Words of an honest, humble, transparent servant. We Christians have received a priceless treasure (the glorious gospel) in a very frail and perishable container (our weak bodies). There is a reason. So nobody will have any question about the source of power, it must be of God and not of any human origin. And so—to verify just how frail our humanity is, Paul lists four common struggles servants live with. I'm calling them consequences. Let's see all four in the two verses that follow before we analyze each one and then expand on them in 2 Corinthians 11. If you have a pencil handy, you might circle the four terms in your Bible: *afflicted, perplexed, persecuted, struck down.*

. . . we are afflicted in every way, but not crushed; perplexed, but not despairing; persecuted, but not forsaken; struck down, but not destroyed (2 Cor. 4:8–9).

Affliction

This word comes from a Greek term that suggests the idea of pressure. This is stress brought on by difficult circumstances or antagonistic people.[1] In other words, when servants are "afflicted," they feel under pressure, harassed, and oppressed. The Greek verb, *thlibo,* is a strong one, meaning at times "to treat with hostility."

Confusion

Paul goes on to say there are times when servants of God become "perplexed." Interestingly, the combination of Greek terms that comprise the original word means "without a way." It is a picture of confusion—not knowing where or to whom to turn for help. Included in the meaning of this word would be such perplexing predicaments as being without necessary resources, feeling embarrassed, and in doubt so far as procedure is concerned. We have the phrase, "at a loss" which adequately describes that uncertain feeling. There is more.

Persecution

Originally, the term persecution meant "to run after, pursue."[2] It's the idea of being chased, having others "on our case," we would say. It is an active, aggressive word conveying everything from being intimidated to being assaulted, actually attacked. Servants *will* suffer persecution. You may recall our discussing this in chapter 8, when we analyzed and applied the last beatitude. Paul comes right out and predicts it *will* happen. "And indeed, all who desire to live godly in Christ Jesus will be persecuted." Persecution is one of those painful consequences, along with affliction and confusion. Finally, he names one more.

Rejection

"Struck down"—this is the idea of being thrown down, shoved aside, or cast off. This explains why J. B. Phillips paraphrases it, ". . . we may be knocked down. . . ." Amazing thing! Even though we may faithfully and consistently do our job, help and serve and give to others, we can expect, on occasion, to be thrown aside and rejected.

A crazy illustration of this occurred to me recently. If you enjoy watching and playing the game of football (I certainly do), you have observed a curious addition in the last several years. It is called a "spike." It's rather unusual. A team fights its way toward the goal line yard by yard. Runs and play-action fakes and passes are mixed in the game plan to catch the defense by surprise. Minutes seem like hours as the offensive team plods along. Suddenly, it happens. A play works beautifully—the defense is out of position—and streaking to the long-awaited touchdown is a muscular running back or some fleet-footed split end. Six points! But as soon as he crosses the line, this athlete takes the ball and *slams* the little thing to the ground. With *all* his might. I mean, that ball bounces like mad as it is mercilessly thrown down. The guy doesn't so much as say, "Thanks, ball."

I've thought, "What if that ball had feeling? What if it could talk?" Can you imagine how it would react after being spiked? It had done its job well. Stayed inflated. Didn't jump out of the player's arms—no fumble. *It* is the reason the team got six points. And after all that, all the thanks it gets is a vicious spike. *Talk about rejection!* So it is with God's servants. We do what is right . . . and we get tossed aside. Sometimes, viciously. It hurts.

Servants, listen up! These four words form an inspired "outline" of the treatment we can expect. These are the consequences—the dark side—of serving. Let's keep our eyes wide open when we grab the towel to do a little one-on-one foot washing. Every once in a while we are going to get kicked. Now, this doesn't mean God has abandoned us or that we are out of His will. It just means people are people, sheep are sheep. It's all part of the humbling process God uses in shaping our lives "to bear the family likeness of His Son" (Rom. 8:29, PHILLIPS).

SPELLING OUT THE CONSEQUENCES

Now—so much for the theory. Let's see how these things impact us in everyday living. Turn to 2 Corinthians 11. The same one who wrote about affliction, confusion, persecution, and rejection in chapter 4 now amplifies each in chapter 11. The fourth chapter tells us what will happen, the eleventh spells out how. But before we see how these chapters fit together, let me show you something interesting. In verse 23 of 2 Corinthians 11, Paul asks: "Are they servants of Christ? . . . I more so." And immediately what does he mention to show that he has a better claim on servanthood than others? The things he *suffered!* Isn't that significant? In the next several verses, Paul lists one painful consequence after another to prove to his readers just how authentic a servant he was. It is an inescapable fact. If you get serious about being shaped into Christ's image, you'll have to learn to cope with the consequences. Those who serve *will* suffer.

Let's read these verses slowly:

> Are they servants of Christ? (I speak as if insane) I more so; in far more labors, in far more imprisonments, beaten times without number, often in danger of death.
>
> Five times I received from the Jews thirty-nine lashes.
>
> Three times I was beaten with rods, once I was stoned, three times I was shipwrecked, a night and a day I have spent in the deep.
>
> I have been on frequent journeys, in dangers from rivers, dangers from robbers, dangers from my countrymen, dangers from the Gentiles, dangers in the city, dangers in the wilderness, dangers on the sea, dangers among false brethren; I have been in labor and hardship, through many sleepless nights, in hunger and thirst, often without food, in cold and exposure.
>
> Apart from such external things, there is the daily pressure upon me of concern for all the churches (2 Cor. 11:23–28).

What stories Paul could tell!

Now, remember the four words from 2 Corinthians 4? Chapter 11, verses 23-28, amplifies each. The comparison looks like this:

Chapter 4	*Chapter 11*
· Affliction	". . . in far more labors"
· Confusion	". . . in far more imprisonments"
· Persecution	". . . beaten times without number"
· Rejection	". . . often in danger of death"

The two are obviously tied together. Each of the four categories of consequences in chapter 4 is spelled out in chapter 11 where a few of the actual events are given.

In Labors

Answering to the pressure-and-stress (affliction) category are the "labors" Paul mentions when he shares:

> I have been in labor and hardship, through many sleepless nights, in hunger and thirst, often without food, in cold and exposure.
> Apart from such external things, there is the daily pressure upon me of concern for all the churches (2 Cor. 11:27–28).

Now *that's* being under pressure. Funny, we seldom think that a great apostle like Paul ever suffered from insomnia, but he did . . . sometimes because of acute deprivations, like hunger, cold, and exposure . . . and sometimes because of his concern for the many ministries to which he had given himself. "Daily pressure" he calls it.

Pressure and stress are cripplers, sometimes killers. I was made aware of this rather forcefully when I read a book *(Executive Survival Manual)* dealing with the stress executives must endure. In a chapter on "Executive Stress," the authors gauge the impact of pressure on people by measuring the stress factor in "life-change units."[3] The greater the number of units, the greater the risk of emotional or physical illness in the ensuing months. For example, they state if you have to endure 200 to 299 life-change units in a given year, the probability of your suffering some kind of illness within the next two years is 50 percent. If it is 300 or more units, it jumps to 80 percent. I was interested to discover the following list of pressure situations and their corresponding life-change units:[4]

1.	Death of spouse	100
2.	Divorce	73
3.	Marital separation from mate	65
4.	Detention in jail or other institution	63
5.	Death of a close family member	63
6.	Major personal injury or illness	53
7.	Marriage	50

8.	Being fired at work	47
9.	Marital reconciliation with mate	45
10.	Retirement from work	45
11.	Major change in the health or behavior of a family member	44
12.	Pregnancy	40
13.	Sexual difficulties	39
14.	Gaining a new family member (e.g., through birth, adoption, oldster moving in, etc.)	39

. . . .

16.	Major change in financial state (e.g., a lot worse off or, a lot better off than usual)	38
17.	Death of a close friend	37

. . . .

23.	Son or daughter leaving home (e.g., marriage, attending college, etc.)	29
24.	In-law troubles	29

. . . .

30.	Troubles with the boss	23
31.	Major change in working hours or conditions	20
32.	Change in residence	20
33.	Changing to a new school	20

. . . .

41.	Vacation	13
42.	Christmas	12
43.	Minor violations of the law (e.g., traffic tickets, jaywalking, disturbing the peace, etc.)	11

Reading what we do of Paul's pressures, we could assume his life-change units must have been 400 or more!

In Imprisonments

Answering to the "confusion" category of consequences, Paul next mentions the disillusioning times of mistreatment and imprisonment. There certainly must have been times he did not know where to turn—or to whom. Doubt and questions might well have haunted him with maddening regularity. Hear again verse 26:

> I have been on frequent journeys, in dangers from rivers, dangers from robbers, dangers from my countrymen, dangers from the Gentiles, dangers in the city, dangers in the wilderness, dangers on the sea, dangers among false brethren.

Here was one of those great men, "too good for this world," being pushed around, threatened, and living on the raw edge of constant danger. Eight times in this single verse Paul uses *kindunos,* a term translated "danger." If you imagine yourself in those many situations—and toss in several imprisonments to boot—you get the feeling of being "strung out," as we say today. Your mind plays tricks on you. You wonder where God is, and you occasionally even doubt God. You get disoriented, "mixed up" inside. And on top of all that is the one most common experience all who have been in prison admit—*profound loneliness.* Mix all that together . . . and you've got the picture.

Those who have read the remarkable story of Corrie ten Boom in *The Hiding Place* [5] have come to love that strong woman of God who emerged from the horrors of World War II with a faith as solid as granite. But another story of similar tragedy by Elie Wiesel gives readers a different perspective on the horror of the holocaust. Wiesel's *Night* will grab you and not let you go. In terse, tightly packed sentences, he describes those scenes and his own confusion as he witnessed (in his teenage years) a chapter of life we would prefer to erase.

This young Jew saw it all. Fellow Jews from his village were stripped of their possessions and loaded into cattle cars, where a third of them died before they reached their destination. He saw babies pitchforked, little children hanged, weak and emaciated men killed by fellow prisoners for a single piece of molded bread. He even saw his mother, his lovely little sister, and all his family disappear into an oven fueled with human flesh. [6]

Wiesel's God was murdered at Birkenbau. Something dear and precious within his soul also died as all his dreams turned to dust.

Francois Mauriac, the Nobel-prizewinning French author, in writing the foreword to Wiesel's book, describes the time he first met Wiesel:

It was then that I understood what had first drawn me to the young Israeli: that look, as of a Lazarus risen from the dead, yet still a prisoner within the grim confines where he had strayed, stumbling among the shameful corpses. For him, Nietzsche's cry expressed an almost physical reality: God is dead, the God of love, of gentleness, of comfort, the God of Abraham, of Isaac, of Jacob, has vanished forevermore, beneath the gaze of this child, in the smoke of a human holocaust exacted by Race, the most voracious of all idols. And how many pious Jews have experienced this death. On that day, horrible even among those days of horror, when the child watched the hanging (yes) of another child, who, he tells us, had the face of a sad angel, he heard someone behind him groan: "Where is God? Where is He? Where can He be now?"[7]

Confusion. Tragic, horrible confusion. Experiences like those we've just read will do that to you. But the vast difference between Corrie ten Boom and Elie Wiesel cannot be ignored. Servants like Corrie ten Boom who endure the consequences victoriously testify of God's precious faithfulness even through days of confusion.

In Beatings

Answering to the "persecution" category, Paul mentions several specific examples:

> Five times I received from the Jews thirty-nine lashes.
> Three times I was beaten with rods, once I was stoned, three times I was shipwrecked, a night and a day I have spent in the deep (2 Cor. 11:24–25).

Can you imagine being beaten "times without number" (v. 23)? I cannot. Here is the awful reality of physical abuse. Few people will ever know such pain to such an extreme. But if you think the man was pretty much alone in it all, get hold of a copy of *Fox's Book of Martyrs*.[8] You will find one account after another of raw, unashamed persecution. There is no way to get around it, God's servants often become scapegoats.

This is true emotionally more frequently than physically. Man's twisted depravity, for some reason, likes to express itself in this way. Take the prophet Daniel, for example. Faithful, efficient, honest, dedicated to the maximum, the man served others with a pure heart. But it backfired on him. According to the sixth chapter of the book that bears his name in the Old Testament, the very people he worked with turned on him. They set out to prove he lacked integrity. Determined to expose the real truth (which they assumed he was hiding), they left no stone unturned. Can you imagine how that hurt? Just listen:

> Then this Daniel began distinguishing himself among the commissioners and satraps because he possessed an extraordinary spirit, and the king planned to appoint him over the entire kingdom.
> Then the commissioners and satraps began trying to find a ground of accusation against Daniel in regard to government affairs; but they could find no ground of accusation or evidence of corruption, inasmuch as he was faithful, and no negligence or corruption was to be found in him (Dan. 6:3–4).

They found nothing. Bible students often emphasize that fact . . . and we should. But for a moment, picture yourself in Daniel's sandals. You are the object of investigation. You hear whisperings about your character. Stories swirl around, calling into question your words, your actions. Every move you make is viewed with suspicion. And yet there is not a shred of truth to it. You have been a model of authenticity, you have devoted yourself to the dual role of helping others and honoring the Lord . . . and this is the thanks you get. I'll tell you, it takes the grace of Almighty God to press on under those circumstances *and* to accept His plan over our own.

It's like the poet's words:

In Acceptance Lieth Peace

He said, "I will forget the dying faces;
The empty places,

They shall be filled again.
O voices moaning deep within me, cease."
But vain the word; vain, vain:
Not in forgetting lieth peace.

He said, "I will crowd action upon action,
The strife of faction
Shall stir me and sustain;
O tears that drown the fire of manhood
cease."
But vain the word; vain, vain:
Not in endeavour lieth peace.

He said, "I will withdraw me and be
quiet,
Why meddle in life's riot?
Shut be my door to pain.
Desire, thou dost befool me, thou shalt
cease."
But vain the word; vain, vain:
Not in aloofness lieth peace.

He said, "I will submit; I am defeated.
God hath depleted
My life of its rich gain.
O futile murmurings, why will ye not cease?"
But vain the word; vain, vain:
Not in submission lieth peace.

He said, "I will accept the breaking sorrow
Which God to-morrow
Will to His son explain."
Then did the turmoil deep within him cease.
Not vain the word, not vain;
For in Acceptance lieth peace.[9]

In Danger of Death

There is one more comparison of consequences between chapters 4 and 11 of 2 Corinthians: "In danger of death" answers to the category of rejection. In 2 Corinthians 4:9, Paul states we are "struck down." And then to illustrate just how close he came to death itself, he mentions the following experiences in chapter eleven of this letter:

- Shipwrecked three times (11:25)
- A day and a night spent in the ocean (11:25)
- Surrounded by constant dangers (11:26)
- Without sufficient food (11:27)
- Being exposed to the elements (11:27)
- Escaping death by being let down a wall in a large basket (11:33).

This was no criminal. The man was innocent of wrong . . . yet he was misunderstood, mistreated, hunted like a wounded deer, and hated by those who once respected him. What happened? How could so much unfair, near-fatal treatment happen to a man like Paul? An even deeper question is this: How could and why would God permit it?

Without sounding glib . . . it was par for the servanthood course. Still is. Paul even admitted that we are:

. . . always carrying about in the body the dying of Jesus, that the life of Jesus also may be manifested in our body.

For we who live are constantly being delivered over to death for Jesus' sake, that the life of Jesus also may be manifested in our mortal flesh. . . .

Therefore we do not lose heart, but though our outer man is decaying, yet our inner man is being renewed day by day.

For momentary, light affliction is producing for us an eternal weight of glory far beyond all comparison, while we look not at the things which are seen, but at the things which are not seen; for the things which are seen are temporal, but the things which are not seen are eternal (2 Cor. 4:10–11, 16–18).

That sounds beautiful, almost poetic. However, it is one thing to read it as black print on a white page, but it's another thing entirely to embrace that mind-set when all hell breaks loose against us.

How does the servant of God cope when the bottom drops out?

Suggestions for Coping with Consequences

I have found great help from two truths God gave me at a time in my life when I was bombarded with a series of unexpected and unfair blows (from my perspective). In my darkest hours these principles become my anchor of stability, my only means of survival. Afflicted, confused, persecuted, and rejected in that situation, I claimed these two truths and held onto them like one beaten by wild waves, strong winds, and pounding rain would grab hold of the mast on a ship at sea. God took me through the consequences and kept me from becoming a bitter man.

Because they worked for me, I pass them on to you. At the risk of sounding simplistic, I would suggest that you not only write them down where you can read them often, but also that you might commit them to memory. The day will come when you will be thankful you did, I assure you. They have scriptural support, but I'll not list all those verses for the sake of brevity and clarity.

Here is the first truth to claim when enduring the consequences of suffering: **Nothing touches me that has not passed through the hands of my heavenly Father. Nothing.** Whatever occurs, God has sovereignly surveyed and approved. We may not know why (we may *never* know why), but we do know our pain is no accident to Him who guides our lives. He is, in no way, surprised by it all. Before it ever touches us, it passes through Him.

The second truth to claim is this: **Everything I endure is designed to prepare me for serving others more effectively. Everything.**

Since my heavenly Father is committed to shaping me into the image of His Son, He knows the ultimate value of this painful experience. It is a necessary part of the preparation process. It is being used to empty our hands of our own resources, our own sufficiency, and turn us back to Him—the faithful Provider. And God knows what will get through to us.

When our older daughter Charissa underwent two eye surgeries, an ordeal I mentioned in my book *Three Steps Forward, Two Steps Back*,[10] I thought the test was over. It wasn't. Late in the summer of 1979, she suffered a severe fall, resulting in a fracture of two vertabrae in her back. During the early part of that episode, her mother and I were forced to wait on the physical outcome. The most difficult discipline in the Christian life, in my opinion, is waiting. But God used that to force us to lean on him . . . to trust Him . . . to believe in Him . . . to release our will and accept His. Words fail to describe the pain of that transfer of wills. Finally, when we made the transfer, empty-handed and totally dependent, Cynthia and I leaned hard on our God. It was a time of *great* stress.

Today, Charissa's broken back has healed. Our daughter is neither paralyzed nor handicapped in any way. She is whole, healthy, energetic, and a very grateful young woman. And—I might add—*all* the Swindolls have learned again the value of being cast upon our God. Admittedly, in the pain of it all, I wrestled with Him. But, looking back, I can clearly see that the process required being emptied of our own strength. God designed the process to equip my family—and especially their dad—to be better servants.

> One by one He took them from me
>   All the things I valued most;
> 'Til I was empty-handed,
>   Every glittering toy was lost.
> And I walked earth's highways, grieving,
>   In my rags and poverty.
> Until I heard His voice inviting,
>   "Lift those empty hands to Me!"

Then I turned my hands toward heaven,
    And He filled them with a store
Of His own transcendent riches,
    'Til they could contain no more.

And at last I comprehended
    With my stupid mind, and dull,
That God cannot pour His riches
    Into hands already full.
                    —Source Unknown

Things may not be logical and fair, but when God is directing the events of our lives, they are right. Even when we suffer the painful consequences of serving others.

13

The Rewards of Serving

So much for the dark side of serving. Let's end on a positive note. Serving *definitely* has rewards, and they are numerous. They far outweigh the consequences. When we think about them, they motivate us to keep going.

One of the great doctrines of Christianity is our firm belief in a heavenly home. Ultimately, we shall spend eternity with God in the place He has prepared for us. And part of that exciting anticipation is His promise to reward His servants for a job well done. I don't know many believers in Jesus Christ who never think of being with their Lord in heaven, receiving His smile of acceptance, and hearing His "well done, good and faithful servant." We even refer to one who died in this way: "He has gone home to his reward." A lot of strange opinions (some weird and wild ideas) surround this subject. But the Bible is fairly clear regarding the rewards of serving. First and foremost, we need to hear what it says.

I remember, as a little boy in a south Texas Baptist church, singing the words:

> I am thinking today of that beautiful land
>   I shall reach when the sun goeth down;
> When through wonderful grace by my Saviour I stand,
>   Will there be any stars in my crown?
>
> Will there be any stars, any stars in my crown
>   When at evening the sun goeth down?
> When I wake with the blest in the mansions of rest,
>   Will there be any stars in my crown?
>   —Eliza E. Hewitt, "Will There Be Any Stars?"

I wondered about that. It seemed spooky, almost unreal. How could stars be in a crown I wore?

Many years later I learned and loved another piece of church music. It came from an old volume of devotional verse bearing the title *Immanuel's Land and Other Pieces* by A. R. C., the initials modestly representing the name of Anne R. Cousin. When she was only thirty-two, the author composed her best-known hymn, "The Sands of Time Are Sinking." The original poem contains nineteen verses,[1] but most Christians are familiar with only four or five. The concluding stanza will always be one of my favorites:

> The bride eyes not her garment,
>   But her dear bridegroom's face;
> I will not gaze at glory,
>   But on my King of grace:
> Not at the crown He giveth,
>   But on His piercéd hand;
> The Lamb is all the glory
>   Of Emmanuel's land.[2]

Both those old songs speak of heavenly crowns. They sound interesting, but what does *the Bible* say? Does Scripture support the idea of tangible rewards?

BIBLICAL FACTS ABOUT REWARDS

In 1 Corinthians 3:10–14 we read:

> According to the grace of God which was given to me, as a wise masterbuilder I laid a foundation, and another is building upon it. But let each man be careful how he builds upon it.
>
> For no man can lay a foundation other than the one which is laid, which is Jesus Christ.
>
> Now if any man builds upon the foundation with gold, silver, precious stones, wood, hay, straw, each man's work will become evident; for the day will show it, because it is to be revealed with fire; and the fire itself will test the quality of each man's work.
>
> If any man's work which he has built upon it remains, he shall receive a reward.

Scripture not only supports the idea of eternal rewards, it spells out the specifics. I find three primary facts about rewards in this section of Scripture:

1. **Most rewards are received in heaven, not on earth.**

Now don't misunderstand. There are earthly rewards. Even the world provides certain people with special honors: the Pulitzer Prize, Nobel Peace Prize, Academy Awards, Emmy, Tony, Grammy . . . and we all know that athletes win All-American honors or All-Pro and the Heisman Trophy. The military also offers medals of bravery, like the Navy Cross, the Purple Heart, the Bronze Star, and the Medal of Honor. But when it comes to servanthood, God reserves special honor for that day when "each man's work will become evident" and "he shall receive a reward" (3:13–14). Most of the rewards servants will receive will be given after death, not before.

2. **All rewards are based on quality, not quantity.**

Did you notice this in those verses from 1 Corinthians? ". . . the fire itself will test the *quality* of each man's work" (emphasis mine).

We humans are impressed with size and volume and noise and numbers. It is easy to forget that God's eye is always on motive, authenticity, the real truth *beneath* the surface, never the external splash. When He rewards servants, it will be based on *quality*—which means everybody has an equal opportunity to receive a reward. The dear older lady who prays will be rewarded as much as the evangelist who preaches to thousands. The quiet, faithful friend who assists another in need will be rewarded as much as the strong natural leader whose gifts are more visible. A cool cup of water given to a hurting soul, bruised with adversity, will be rewarded as much as an act of sacrifice on the mission field. God, our faithful Lord, promises to reward the quality of our work. The glory may be postponed until eternity, but it will come, which leads me into the third fact about rewards.

3. **No reward that is postponed will be forgotten.**
Make no mistake about it, the Bible clearly teaches ". . . he shall receive a reward." God doesn't settle His accounts at the end of every day. Nor does He close out His books toward the end of everyone's life. No, not then. But be assured, fellow servant, when that day in eternity dawns, when time shall be no more on this earth, no act of serving others—be it well-known or unknown by others—will be forgotten.

A nineteenth-century senator, Benjamin Hill, spoke with eloquence when he made this fitting tribute to Confederate General Robert E. Lee (a great man with a servant's spirit):

> He was a foe without hate, a friend without treachery, a soldier without cruelty, and a victim without murmuring. He was a public officer without vices, a private citizen without wrong, a neighbor without reproach, a Christian without hypocrisy, and a man without guilt. He was Caesar without his ambition, Frederick without his tyranny, Napoleon without his selfishness, and Washington without his reward.[2]

And the marvelous part of it all is that you don't have to be a Robert E. Lee to be remembered. You don't have to be a courageous soldier in battle or a statesman who graciously accepts defeat. You can be a "nobody" in the eyes of this world and your faithful God will, someday, reward your every act of servanthood. Rewards may be postponed, but they will not be forgotten forever. Unlike many people today, God keeps His promises.

GOD'S PROMISES TO HIS SERVANTS

Someone once counted all the promises in the Bible and came up with an amazing figure of almost 7500. Among that large number are some specific promises servants can claim today. Believe me, there are times the only hope to keep you going will be in something God has declared in His Word, promising that your work is not in vain. Let's divide these promises into two groups—those that have to do with *His* faithfulness and those that have to do with *our* faithfulness.

Regarding His Faithfulness

I want to mention several helpful promises that assure us of God's sticking by us before I pinpoint one in particular that deserves special attention.

Isaiah 41:10 has often encouraged me:

> Do not fear, for I am with you;
> Do not anxiously look about you, for I am your God.
> I will strengthen you, surely I will help you,
> Surely I will uphold you with my righteous right hand.

And a little further on, Isaiah writes:

> But Zion said, "The Lord has forsaken me,
> And the Lord has forgotten me."
> "Can a woman forget her nursing child,
> And have no compassion on the son of her womb?
> Even these may forget, but I will not forget you.
> "Behold, I have inscribed you on the palms of My hands;
> Your walls are continually before Me . . ." (Isa. 49:14–16).

Isn't that fantastic! More faithful than a nursing mother, our God watches over and cares about us.

We have frequently received counsel from Paul the apostle. Let's look now at a few of the promises God led Him to write. In 2 Corinthians 4:16–18 we read:

> Therefore we do not lose heart, but though our outer man is decaying, yet our inner man is being renewed day by day.
> For momentary, light affliction is producing for us an eternal weight of glory far beyond all comparison.

And who can forget Philippians 4:19?

> And my God shall supply all your needs according to His riches in glory in Christ Jesus.

Or his words of hope regarding a choice servant named Onesiphorus?

> The Lord grant mercy to the house of Onesiphorus, for he often refreshed me, and was not ashamed of my chains; but when he was in Rome, he eagerly searched for me, and found me—the Lord grant to him to find mercy from the Lord on that day—and you know very well what services he rendered at Ephesus (2 Tim. 1:16–18).

No, our faithful God will never forget His own. Perhaps the most well-known promises Christians have as their ultimate hope are in Revelation 21:1–4:

> And I saw a new heaven and a new earth; for the first heaven and the first earth passed away, and there is no longer any sea.
> And I saw the holy city, new Jerusalem, coming down out of heaven from God, made ready as a bride adorned for her husband.
> And I heard a loud voice from the throne, saying, "Behold, the tabernacle of God is among men, and He shall dwell among them, and they shall be His people, and God Himself shall be among them, and He shall wipe away every tear from their eyes;

and there shall no longer be any death; there shall no longer be any mourning, or crying, or pain; the first things have passed away."

And Revelation 22:3–5:

And there shall no longer be any curse; and the throne of God and of the Lamb shall be in it, and His bond-servants shall serve Him; and they shall see His face, and His name shall be on their foreheads.

And there shall no longer be any night; and they shall not have need of the light of a lamp nor the light of the sun, because the Lord God shall illumine them; and they shall reign forever and ever.

Magnificent, incredible, unchanging hope drips from those immortal words. I encourage you to mark them well. There will be thankless days and long nights when these promises will get you through.

But of all the promises of God's faithfulness in taking special note of His servants, one stands out as my favorite—Hebrews 6:10, which reads:

For God is not unjust so as to forget your work and the love which you have shown toward His name, in having ministered and in still ministering to the saints.

I like the way *The Living Bible* reads:

For God is not unfair. How can he forget your hard work for him, or forget the way you used to show your love for him—and still do—by helping his children?

The writer is talking to Christians. The word *beloved* in the previous verse assures us of that. And he is writing out of concern for a few of the first-century believers who had begun to cool off and drift from a close walk with God. He wants to encourage them to stay at it, to keep going, to count on the Lord their God to take notice of them and reward them accordingly. In other words, he reminds them of that great truth all of us tend to forget when days turn into a slow grind, *God is faithful!* He uses eight words to convey this fact: "... *God is not unjust so as to forget....*"

What does it mean to say that God is faithful? It means He is steadfast in His allegiance to His people. He will not leave us in the lurch. It also means He is firm in His adherence to His promises. He keeps His word. Faithfulness suggests the idea of loyalty; dependability; constancy; being resolute, steady, and consistent. God isn't fickle, no hot-and-cold temperamental moods with Him!

And then the verse goes on to tell us what God faithfully remembers about His servants:

1. He remembers our work—each individual act.
2. He also takes note of the love within us that prompted the deed.

No one on earth can do those special things. We forget, but God remembers. We see the action, God sees the motive. This qualifies Him as the best record keeper and judge. He alone is perfectly and consistently just. Servants, you're in good hands with the Almighty!

Even the best of servants get weary. The Lord's desire is to encourage us to be diligent and to trust Him in spite of the demands. That is why this same writer, before the ink is dry on verse 10, adds:

> And we are anxious that you keep right on loving others as long as life lasts, so that you will get your full reward.
>
> Then, knowing what lies ahead for you, you won't become bored with being a Christian, nor become spiritually dull and indifferent, but you will be anxious to follow the example of those who receive all that God has promised them because of their strong faith and patience (Heb. 6:11–12 TLB).

Regarding Our Faithfulness

In several places through the New Testament, there are statements of promise from God to faithful servants. Three stand out in my mind:

> So, my dear brothers, since future victory is sure, be strong and steady, always abounding in the Lord's work, for you know that nothing you do for the Lord is ever wasted as it would be if there were no resurrection (1 Cor. 15:58, TLB).

Underscore "wasted." It's another way of saying, "Your work is not in vain."

> And let us not lose heart in doing good, for in due time we shall reap if we do not grow weary.
> So then, while we have opportunity, let us do good to all men, and especially to those who are of the household of the faith (Gal. 6:9–10).

Underscore "we shall reap."

> With good will render service, as to the Lord, and not to men, knowing that whatever good thing each one does, this he will receive back from the Lord, whether slave or free (Eph. 6:7–8).

Underscore "he will receive back."

When we have done what was needed, but were ignored, misunderstood, or forgotten . . . we can be sure it was NOT IN VAIN. When we did what was right, with the right motive, but received no credit, no acknowledgment, not even a "thank you" . . . we have God's promise WE SHALL REAP. When any servant has served and given and sacrificed and then willingly stepped aside for God to receive the glory, our heavenly Father promises HE WILL RECEIVE BACK.

To be even more specific, God has organized His "reward

system" into a unique arrangement. He offers His servants both temporal and eternal rewards.

Temporal Rewards

Back into the familiar territory of 2 Corinthians 4, read again verses 7 through 11:

> But we have this treasure in earthen vessels, that the surpassing greatness of the power may be of God and not from ourselves; we are afflicted in every way, but not crushed; perplexed, but not despairing; persecuted, but not forsaken; struck down, but not destroyed; always carrying about in the body the dying of Jesus, that the life of Jesus also may be manifested in our body.
>
> For we who live are constantly being delivered over to death for Jesus' sake, that the life of Jesus also may be manifested in our mortal flesh.

I'll be candid with you, I have never read anywhere else what God recently revealed to me in the latter half of this Scripture (vv. 10–11), which follows on the heels of what we might call the "painful side" of serving (vv. 7–9). Let me emphasize verses 10 and 11 by recording the way another version renders them:

> We always carry around in our body the death of Jesus, so that the life of Jesus may also be revealed in our body. For we who are alive are always being given over to death for Jesus' sake, so that his life may be revealed in our mortal body (NIV).

Do you observe the temporal reward woven into the lines of those verses? It is this: *The quiet awareness that the life of Christ is being modeled.* That is part of what Paul means when he writes, ". . . that the life of Jesus may also be revealed in our body." Frankly, I know of few more satisfying and encouraging rewards than the deep realization that our actions (and the motives behind them) are visible expressions of Christ to others.

There is one more temporal reward mentioned in this same section of 2 Corinthians:

> All this is for your benefit, so that the grace that is reaching more and more people may cause thanksgiving to overflow to the glory of God (v. 15, NIV).

It's not hidden. The Lord comes up front and says that when you and I take the role of a servant, there is *the joyful realization that a thankful spirit is being stimulated.* And, please notice in verse 15, God gets the glory. It overflows!

I mentioned in chapter 11 the man in our church who quietly and graciously washed our windows. Do you know what pervaded our home throughout that entire Christmas season? A thankful spirit. It washed over all of us in the family. Every glance at another clean window created within us a grateful heart.

Consider also the exhausting efforts of mothers with babies and toddlers. I cannot think of a more thankless task than caring for the young week in, week out . . . month after tiring month. But mothers, hear me well! Your servant's spirit has an effect on all your family. And there are those special times when you go far beyond the expected call of duty.

I was reminded of a perfect example of this while reading Joyce Landorf's splendid work, *Mourning Song.* Joyce is a close, personal friend of mine. She has written many fine books, but nothing better, in my opinion, than this courageous and eloquent account of the death of her mother. In dealing with the subject of pain and suffering in the hospital, Joyce tells of another mother whose significance cannot be exaggerated—a woman whose story illustrates how one who serves can change the entire atmosphere of a room. Take the time to read and feel the emotion in Joyce's own words:

> Nurses carry out their various duties with callous indifference. They listen as little as possible and touch only when necessary. How sad, but such is the force of denial.
>
> It's as if they do indeed hear the mourning song, but they run blindly from the sound, holding their ears as they run and hoping none of the message will get through their carefully structured blockades.

I have seen the terminally ill children in several hospitals and I can fully appreciate how soul-tearing it is to try and work around them. However, it still is tragic to let denial rob us of feeling, caring, and loving the dying child.

My co-worker, Dr. James Dobson, told me of a mother who was willing to put down her denial, pick up her own acceptance, and then beautifully prepare her little son for his death.

She was a large, black woman, as picturesque as the plantation mammies of years ago. She came every day to the hospital to visit her little five-year-old son who was dying of the painful disease lung cancer.

One morning, before the mother got there, a nurse heard the little boy saying, "I hear the bells! I hear the bells! They're ringing!" Over and over that morning nurses and staff heard him.

When the mother arrived she asked one of the nurses how her son had been that day, and the nurse replied, "Oh, he's hallucinating today—it's probably the medication, but he's not making any sense. He keeps on saying he hears bells."

Then that beautiful mother's face came alive with understanding, and she shook her finger at the nurse and said, "You listen to me. He is not hallucinating and he's not out of his head because of any medicine. I told him weeks ago that when the pain in his chest got bad and it was hard to breathe, it meant he was going to leave us. It meant he was going to go to heaven—and that when the pain got really bad he was to look up into the corner of his room—towards heaven—and listen for the bells of heaven—because they'd be ringing for him!" With that, she marched down that hall, swept into her little son's room, swooped him out of his bed, and rocked him in her arms until the sounds of ringing bells were only quiet echoes, and he was gone.[3]

You'll never convince me that that great woman in her gallant act of mothering did not leave the hospital a different place from what she found it! The role of serving may seem insignificant . . . but, in reality, it is *dynamite*.

Eternal Rewards

On top of these temporal benefits connected to serving, there are eternal rewards as well. Christ Himself, while preparing the

Twelve for a lifetime of serving others, promised an eternal reward even for holding out a cup of cool water. Listen:

"He who receives a prophet in the name of a prophet shall receive a prophet's reward; and he who receives a righteous man in the name of a righteous man shall receive a righteous man's reward.

"And whoever in the name of a disciple gives to one of these little ones even a cup of cold water to drink, truly I say to you he shall not lose his reward" (Matt. 10:41–42).

Those words tell us that "improving our serve" begins with little things. It begins with thoughtful things—an understanding embrace of one who is hurting, a brief note to one who is lonely and feeling unappreciated and forgotten, a cup of cool water for one whose lips are parched from the hot blast of a barren desert when all seems futile and worthless. God takes special notice of all these efforts.

These words take on a new shade of significance when we read that familiar account in Matthew 25. The scene is after this life. The Judge is offering His rewards. The servants receiving them were so unselfish, they had long since forgotten the deeds. But not our Lord!

"But when the Son of Man comes in His glory, and all the angels with Him, then He will sit on His glorious throne.

"And all the nations will be gathered before Him; and He will separate them from one another, as the shepherd separates the sheep from the goats;

and He will put the sheep on His right, and the goats on the left.

"Then the King will say to those on His right, 'Come you who are blessed of My Father, inherit the kingdom prepared for you from the foundation of the world.

'For I was hungry, and you gave Me something to eat; I was thirsty, and you gave Me drink; I was a stranger, and you invited Me in; naked, and you clothed Me; I was sick, and you visited Me; I was in prison, and you came to Me.'

"Then the righteous will answer Him, saying, 'Lord, when did we see You hungry, and feed You, or thirsty, and give You drink?

'And when did we see You a stranger, and invite You in, or naked, and clothe You?

'And when did we see You sick, or in prison, and come to You?'

"And the King will answer and say to them, 'Truly I say to you, to the extent that you did it to one of these brothers of Mine, even the least of them, you did it to Me'" (Matt. 25:31–40).

Crowns

This chapter would be incomplete if I failed to mention the eternal "crowns" being set aside for God's servants. What an intriguing study! But for our purpose here, I will simply list the eternal crowns mentioned in the New Testament and offer a brief explanation of each. There are at least five crowns promised in the Bible:

1. **The Imperishable Crown** (1 Cor. 9:24–27).

This reward is promised to those who victoriously run the race of life. Taking into consideration verses 26 and 27, that is, the "buffeting" of the body, it is clear that this reward will be awarded those believers who consistently bring the flesh under the Holy Spirit's control, refusing to be enslaved by their sinful nature. In other words, those who carry out the truths of Romans 6:6–14.

2. **The Crown of Exultation** (Phil. 4:1; 1 Thess. 2:19–20).

This crown will be one over which its recipients will glory and rejoice! This is the "soul-winners crown." It is claimed by Paul regarding two bodies of believers whom he had led to and discipled in Christ Jesus . . . the Philippians and the Thessalonians. Our Lord will distribute this crown to those servants who are faithful to declare the gospel, lead souls to Christ, and build them up in Him. And remember—the rewards at this judgment will be based on the *quality* not *quantity* of our earthly works (1 Cor. 3:13).

3. The Crown of Righteousness (2 Tim. 4:7–8).

The crown of righteousness will be awarded those who live each day, loving and anticipating Christ's imminent return . . . those who conduct their earthly lives with eternity's value in view. Kenneth Wuest captures the complete meaning of verse 8 with these words:

> To those who have considered precious His appearing and therefore have loved it, and as a result at the present time are still holding that attitude in their hearts, to those the Lord Jesus will also give the victor's garland of righteousness.[4]

Those who qualify for this crown anxiously look for His return daily.

4. The Crown of Life (James 1:12).

This wonderful reward awaits those saints who suffered in a noble manner during their earthly life. The significance of this reward is not only related to the words *perseveres under trial* but also the words *those who love Him.* This crown is not promised simply to those who endure suffering and trials . . . but to those who endure their trials, loving the Savior all the way! Therefore, loving the Lord and having the desire that He be glorified in and through the trials become the dual motive for the believer's endurance. Those saints who qualify (and the Lord is the Judge!) will receive the crown of life.

5. The Crown of Glory (1 Pet. 5:1–4).

This reward is promised to those who faithfully "shepherd the flock" in keeping with the requirements spelled out in verses 2 and 3. Those under-shepherds who fulfill these qualifications (willingness, sacrificial dedication, humility, an exemplary life) will receive this crown of glory.

After receiving these crowns, what then? Listen to Revelation 4:9–11:

> And when the living creatures give glory and honor and thanks to Him who sits on the throne, to Him who lives forever and ever, the twenty-four elders will fall down before Him who sits on the throne, and will worship Him who lives forever and ever, and will cast their crowns before the throne, saying, "Worthy art

Thou, our Lord and our God, to receive glory and honor and power; for Thou didst create all things, and because of Thy will they existed, and were created."

What a scene! All God's servants are before His throne. What are they doing? Strutting around heaven displaying their crowns? No. Separated from one another, like peacocks, proudly displaying their tangible trophies? No. The servants are bowing in worship, having cast all crowns before their Lord in adoration and praise, ascribing worth and honor to the only One deserving of praise—the Lord God!

ENCOURAGEMENT TO SERVANTS

We have covered a lot of scriptural territory in this chapter. What began as a simple promise that God will reward us became a rather involved analysis of what, how, when, and why. Perhaps three or four thoughts will help put all of this in proper perspective.

First, every act of servanthood—no matter how small or large—will be remembered by God.

Second, He takes special note of the heart—He knows the love behind our actions.

Third, as servants reach out to others, Christ's life is modeled and a spirit of thankfulness is stimulated.

Fourth, special and specific rewards are reserved in heaven for those who practice the art of unselfish living.

It was well-known author and pastor Charles Allen who first told the story of a little lad named John Todd, born in Rutland, Vermont, in the autumn of 1800. Shortly after the boy's birth, the Todd family moved to the little village of Killingsworth. It was there, when John was only six, that both his parents died. All the children had to be parceled out among relatives—and a kind-hearted aunt who lived ten miles away agreed to take John, to love him, to care for him, and to give him a home.

The boy lived there for some fifteen years and finally left as he went on to school to study for the ministry. Time passed gently as he began and later excelled in his work as a pastor. While he was in middle life, his elderly aunt fell desperately ill. Realizing death was not far off, in great distress she wrote her nephew. The pitiful letter included some of the same questions all of us must one day ask: "What will death be like? Will it mean the end of everything?" Fear and uncertainty were easily traced in the quivering lines of her letter.

Moved with compassion and swamped with the memories of yesteryear, he wrote her these words of reassurance:

It is now thirty-five years since I, a little boy of six, was left quite alone in the world. You sent me word you would give me a home and be a kind mother to me. I have never forgotten the day when I made the long journey of ten miles to your house in North Killingsworth. I can still recall my disappointment when, instead of coming for me yourself, you sent your colored man, Caesar, to fetch me. I well remember my tears and my anxiety as, perched high on your horse and clinging tight to Caesar, I rode off to my new home. Night fell before we finished the journey and as it grew dark, I became lonely and afraid.

"Do you think she'll go to bed before I get there?" I asked Caesar anxiously. "O no," he said reassuringly. "She'll sure stay up FOR YOU. When we get out of these here woods you'll see her candle shining in the window." Presently we did ride out in the clearing and there, sure enough, was your candle. I remember you were waiting at the door, that you put your arms close about me and that you lifted me—a tired and bewildered little boy—down from the horse. You had a big fire burning on the hearth, a hot supper waiting for me on the stove. After supper, you took me to my new room, you heard me say my prayers and then you sat beside me until I fell asleep.

You probably realize why I am recalling all this to your memory. Some day soon, God will send for you, to take you to a new home. Don't fear the summons—the strange journey—or the dark messenger of death. God can be trusted to do as much for you as you were kind enough to do for me so many years ago. At the end of the road you will find love and a welcome waiting, and you will be safe in God's care. I shall watch you and pray for you until you are out of sight, and then wait for the day when I shall

make the journey myself and find you waiting at the end of the
road to greet me.[5]

I can hardly read those words without choking back the tears.
Not only is it a beautiful, true story, it is the hope of all who
serve. It is the way it will be. It is the "Well done, good and
faithful servant" we shall hear. As the letter indicates, we are
expected. He is waiting to welcome us. To those who serve, to
those who stand where Jesus Christ once stood many, many
years ago, He promises a reward. And we can be sure He will
keep his promise.

Conclusion

The art of unselfish living is practiced by few and mastered by even fewer. In the fast-paced world of the 1980s, we shouldn't be surprised. It is difficult to cultivate a servant's heart when you are trying to survive in a chaotic society dominated by selfish pursuits. And the greatest tragedy of such an existence is what it spawns: an independent, self-sufficient, survival-of-the-fittest mentality. As I view the future, I see nothing on the horizon that offers any hope for a change. Nothing external, that is. Grim as it may sound, we are on a collision course, and the travelers are both lonely and confused. Some are downright angry.

They offer cynical advice: "Look, you can't change the world. Just look out for number one, hold on, and keep your mouth shut." We are surrounded by those who embrace this philosophy. I admit there are times in my more hurried and hassled moments when I tend to listen to that counsel. And often those who do listen become successful—adding weight to their words.

But this philosophy doesn't satisfy. Surely man was not designed to live and treat others like that. There *has* to be a better way to enter eternity than being cold-hearted, empty-handed, and out of breath!

There is. I have been writing about it for thirteen chapters.

As you have discovered, however, the principles I have discussed must be implemented from within. They are unlike anything you'll hear from self-made superstars and celebrities whose lifestyles are not compatible with the concept of being a servant. That's to be expected. But you are different. You wouldn't have read this far if you weren't. Unless I miss my guess, you are tired of the superficial. You want to be a force for good in a world of evil—a person of authenticity in a world of hypocrisy. You are tired of just criticizing what you see happening around you—you want to be part of the answer, not part of the problem. You appreciate, as I do, these words of a wise old professor:

> There is a new problem in our country. We are becoming a nation that is dominated by large institutions—churches, businesses, governments, labor unions, universities—and these big institutions are not serving us well. I hope that all of you will be concerned about this. Now you can do as I do, stand outside and criticize, bring pressure if you can, write and argue about it. All of this may do some good. But nothing of substance will happen unless there are people inside these institutions who are able to (and want to) lead them into better performance for the public good. Some of you ought to make careers inside these big institutions and become a force for good—from the inside.[1]

All the way through this book, I have stated and reaffirmed the same, essential point: Since Jesus Christ, the Son of God, took upon Himself the role of a servant, so must we. The One who could have been or done anything, consciously and voluntarily, chose to be one who served, one who gave. So then, if we are to become increasingly more like Christ (that is still our goal, isn't it?) then we, too, are to give and to serve.

Enough has been written about it. It is time to put these words and principles to use . . . to hammer them out on the anvil of where we live and work and play. If they work there, the truth of this book will have no trouble withstanding those who say, "It won't work, so don't waste your time." But if they fail to produce the kind of men and women who model the life of Jesus Christ, I have been sadly and grossly misled.

Time will prove the value of these truths on servanthood. May God honor His name as you and I commit ourselves anew to improving our serve, to cultivating the art of unselfish living, serving and giving to others.

Like Jesus Christ.

Notes

Chapter One

1. See Frank Sartwell, "The Small Satanic Worlds of John Calhoun," *Smithsonian Magazine*, April 1970, p. 68 ff. Also see John B. Calhoun, "The Lemmings' Periodic Journeys Are Not Unique," *Smithsonian Magazine*, January 1971, especially p. 11.
2. Margery Williams, *The Velveteen Rabbit* (New York: Doubleday and Company, Inc., 1958), pp. 16–17.

Chapter Two

1. Visual Products Division/3M, St. Paul, MN 55101.
2. Wilbur Rees, "$3.00 Worth of God," *When I Relax I Feel Guilty* by Tim Hansel (Elgin, IL: David C. Cook Publishing Co., 1979), p. 49.
3. Paul Zimmerman, "He's a Man, Not a Myth," *Sports Illustrated*, 53, no. 4 (July 21, 1980): 61.

4. J. Grant Howard, *The Trauma of Transparency* (Portland: Multnomah Press, 1979), p. 30.
5. J. B. Phillips, *When God Was Man* (Nashville: Abingdon Press, 1955), pp. 26–27.
6. Juan Carlos Ortiz, *Disciple* (Wheaton, IL: Creation House, 1975), pp. 34–35.

Chapter Three

1. S. Lewis Johnson, Jr., "Beware of Philosophy," *Bibliotheca Sacra*, 119, no. 476 (October-December, 1962): 302–303.
2. Reprinted from *Tell Me Again, Lord, I Forget* by Ruth Harms Calkin © 1974 David C. Cook Publishing Co., Elgin, IL 60120. Used by permission.
3. Alexander Whyte, D. D., *Bible Characters*, vol. 2., *The New Testament* (London: Oliphants Ltd., 1952), p. 190.
4. Marion Leach Jacobsen, *Crowded Pews and Lonely People* (Wheaton, IL: Tyndale House Publishers, 1972), p. 110.

Chapter Four

1. Horatio G. Spafford, "It Is Well with My Soul," copyright 1918 The John Church Co. Used by permission of the publisher.
2. G. Abbott-Smith, *A Manual Greek Lexicon of the New Testament* (Edinburgh: T. & T. Clark, 1921), p. 109.
3. G. Kittle, ed., *Theological Dictionary of the New Testament*, vol. 1 (Grand Rapids: Wm. B. Eerdmans Publishing Co., 1964), p. 253.
4. C. M. Battersby, "An Evening Prayer," copyright 1911 by Charles H. Gabriel. © renewed 1939, The Rodeheaver Co. (a div. of Word, Inc.). Used by permission.
5. Charles Caldwell Ryrie, *The Ryrie Study Bible: The New Testament* (Chicago: Moody Press, 1977), p. 56.

6. Ray C. Stedman, "Breaking the Resentment Barrier" (sermon delivered to Peninsula Bible Church, Palo Alto, CA, *Treasures of the Parable* Series, Message 11, July 13, 1969), p. 6.
7. Amy Carmichael, taken from *If,* copyrighted material, p. 48. Used by permission of the Christian Literature Crusade, Fort Washington, PA. 19034.

Chapter Five

1. Leslie B. Flynn, *Great Church Fights* (Wheaton, IL: Victor Books, a division of SP Publications, Inc., 1976), p. 91.
2. Ibid., p. 85.
3. Earl D. Radmacher, *You and Your Thoughts, The Power of Right Thinking* (Wheaton, IL: Tyndale House Publishers, Inc., 1977), pp. 15, 19.
4. A Merriam-Webster, *Webster's New Collegiate Dictionary* (Springfield, MA: G. & C. Merriam Company, 1974), p. 451.
5. Howard Butt, *The Velvet Covered Brick* (San Francisco: Harper & Row, Publishers, 1973), pp. 41–43.
6. John Edmund Haggai, *How to Win Over Worry* (Grand Rapids: Zondervan Publishing House, 1976), pp. 95–96.

Chapter Six

1. Jack Sparks, *The Mind Benders* (Nashville: Thomas Nelson, Inc., Publishers, 1977), pp. 16, 17.
2. Christopher Edwards, *Crazy for God* (Englewood Cliffs, NJ: Prentice-Hall, Inc., 1979).
3. Ronald M. Enroth, "The Power Abusers," *Eternity* October 1979, p. 25.
4. W. E. Vine, *An Expository Dictionary of New Testament Words* (London: Oliphants Ltd., 1940), p. 113.

5. Larry Christenson, *The Renewed Mind* (Minneapolis: Bethany Fellowship, Inc., 1974), p. 41.
6. Dale E. Galloway, *Dream a New Dream* (Wheaton, IL: Tyndale House Publishers, Inc., 1975), pp. 77–78.
7. Reprinted with permission of Macmillan Publishing Co., Inc. from *Creative Brooding* by Robert A. Raines. Copyright © 1966 by Robert A. Raines.

Chapter Seven

1. Jerry White, *Honesty, Morality, & Conscience* (Colorado Springs, CO: NavPress, 1979), pp. 81, 82.
2. William Barclay, *The Gospel of Matthew*, (Edinburgh: The Saint Andrew Press, 1956), 1:86.
3. Augustus M. Toplady, "Rock of Ages, Cleft for Me," (1776).
4. "Man a Nothing," taken from *The Valley of Vision: A Collection of Puritan Prayers and Devotions*, Arthur Bennett, ed., (London: The Banner of Truth Trust, 1975), p. 91.
5. Bernard of Clairvaux, "Jesus, Thou Joy of Loving Hearts," trans. by Ray Palmer.
6. Dag Hammarskjöld, *Markings* (New York: Alfred A. Knopf, 1978), p. 53.
7. Archibald Thomas Robertson, *Word Pictures in the New Testament*, vol. 1 (Nashville: Broadman Press, 1930), p. 41.

Chapter Eight

1. William Barclay, *The Gospel of Matthew*, (Edinburgh: The Saint Andrew Press, 1956) 1:98.
2. Leslie Flynn, *Great Church Fights* (Wheaton, IL: Victor Books a division of SP Publications, Inc., 1976), p. 44.

Chapter Nine

1. Tim Timmons, *Maximum Living in a Pressure-Cooker World* (Waco: Word Books Publisher, 1979), p. 163.
2. "The Battered Wife: What's Being Done?" *Los Angeles Times*, April 27, 1978.
3. Catherine Marshall, *Mr. Jones, Meet the Master* (New York: Fleming H. Revell Company, 1951), pp. 147, 148.
4. John R. W. Stott, *Christian Counter-Culture* (Downers Grove, IL: InterVarsity Press, 1978), pp. 58–59.
5. R. V. G. Tasker, ed., *The Tyndale New Testament Commentaries, The Gospel According to St. Matthew* (Grand Rapids: Wm. B. Eerdmans Publishing Company, 1978), p. 63.
6. Harry Blamires, *The Christian Mind* (Ann Arbor: Servant Books, 1963), p. 3.
7. Rebecca Manley Pippert, *Out of the Salt-Shaker & into the World* (Downers Grove, IL: InterVarsity Press, 1979).
8. John R. W. Stott, *Christian Counter-Culture*, p. 61.
9. D. Martyn Lloyd-Jones, *Studies in the Sermon on the Mount*, vol. 1 (Grand Rapids: Wm. B. Eerdmans Publishing Company, 1959), p. 178.
10. Rebecca Manley Pippert, pp. 125–126.

Chapter Ten

1. J. Oswald Sanders, *Spiritual Leadership* (Chicago: Moody Press, 1967), p. 142.
2. Ibid., pp. 142, 143.
3. Dr. James C. Dobson, *Straight Talk to Men and Their Wives* (Waco: Word Books Publisher, 1980). pp. 58–60.
4. C. S. Lewis, *The Four Loves* (New York: Harcourt, Brace & World, Inc., 1960), p. 169.
5. E. Margaret Clarkson, "So Send I You," copyright © 1954 by Singspiration, Inc. All rights reserved. Used by permission of Singspiration, Inc., Grand Rapids.

Chapter Eleven

1. Wilbur Smith, *Have You Considered Him?* (Downers Grove, IL: InterVarsity Press, 1970), p. 5.
2. Taken from *The Encyclopedia of Religious Quotations*, Frank Mead, ed., (Old Tappen, NJ: Fleming H. Revell, n.d.), p. 51.
3. Ibid., p. 56.
4. James "Frog" Sullivan, *The Frog Who Never Became a Prince* (Santa Ana, CA: Vision House Publishers, 1975), pp. 127–131.

Chapter Twelve

1. W. E. Vine, *Expository Dictionary of New Testament Words*, vol. 1 (London: Oliphants Ltd., 1970), p. 38.
2. W. E. Vine, *Expository Dictionary of New Testament Words*, vol. 3 (London: Oliphants Ltd., 1970), pp. 177–178.
3. Thomas V. Bonoma and Dennis P. Slevin, ed., *Executive Survival Manual* (Boston: CBI Publishing Company, Inc., 1978), pp. 58–59.
4. Reprinted with permission from *Journal of Psychosomatic Research*, vol. 11, T. H. Homes and R. H. Rahe, "The Social Readjustment Rating Scale," Copyright 1967, Pergamon Press, Ltd.
5. Corrie ten Boom, *The Hiding Place* (Minneapolis: A Chosen Book published for World Wide Pictures, 1971).
6. Elie Wiesel, *Night* (New York: Avon Books, 1969), p. 9.
7. Ibid.
8. Wm. Byron Forbush, ed., *Fox's Book of Martyrs* (Philadelphia: Universal Book and Bible House, 1926).
9. Amy Carmichael, "In Acceptance Lieth Peace" taken from *Toward Jerusalem* (copyright 1936), pp. 40–41. Used by permission of the Christian Literature Crusade, Fort Washington, PA 19034.
10. Charles R. Swindoll, *Three Steps Forward, Two Steps Back* (Nashville: Thomas Nelson Publishers, 1980).

Chapter Thirteen

1. Richard H. Seume, comp. and ed., *Hymns of Jubilee*, (Dallas: Dallas Theological Seminary, n.d.), p. 49.
2. John Bartlett, ed., *Familiar Quotations* (Boston: Little, Brown and Company, 1955), p. 660.
3. Joyce Landorf, *Mourning Song* (Old Tappan, NJ: Fleming H. Revell Company, 1974), pp. 52–53.
4. Kenneth S. Wuest, *The Pastoral Epistles in the Greek New Testament* (Grand Rapids: Wm. B. Eerdmans Publishing Co., 1956), p. 163.
5. Charles L. Allen, *You Are Never Alone* (Old Tappan, NJ: Fleming H. Revell Company, 1978), pp. 77–79.

Conclusion

1. Robert K. Greenleaf, *Servant Leadership* (New York: Paulist Press, 1977), pp. 1–2.

Other Word Products by Charles R. Swindoll

BIBLE STUDY GUIDES

A Ministry Anyone Could Trust
  (II Corinthians)
A Ministry Everyone Would
  Respect (II Corinthians)
Abraham
Beholding Christ, The Lamb of
  God (John 15–21)
Calm Answers, I Corinthians
Christ's Agony and Ecstasy
Coming to Terms with Sin
Contagious Christianity
Daniel
David
Dropping Your Guard
Exalting Christ, The Son of God
  (John 1–5)
Following Christ, The Man of
  God (John 6–14)
Galatians: Letter of Liberation
Growing Pains
Growing Up in God's Family
Hand Me Another Brick
Improving Your Serve
Issues and Answers
  (formerly Questions Christians
  Ask)

Jesus, Our Lord
Joseph: From Pit to Pinacle
Koinonia
Lamentations of Jeremiah
Learning to Walk by Grace
Letters to Churches
Living on the Ragged Edge
Moses
Living Above the Level of
  Mediocrity
New Testament Postcards
Old Testament Characters
Practical Helps, I Corinthians
Practical Life of Faith
Preeminent Person of Christ
Prophecy
Questions Christians Ask
Relating to Others in Love
Solomon
Spiritual Gifts
Steadfast Christianity
Stones of Remembrance
Strengthening Your Grip
Strong Reproofs, I Corinthians
You and Your Child
You and Your Problems

BOOKTRAX (Books on Cassette)

Improving Your Serve
Living Above the Level of Mediocrity
Living Beyond the Daily Grind, Book 1
Living Beyond the Daily Grind, Book 2
Living on the Ragged Edge
Strengthening Your Grip

VIDEO AND FILMS

People of Refuge. This single film provides practical examples for the church to become genuinely compassionate and friendly to the lonely and distress. Available on video cassette and 16mm film.

Strengthening Your Grip. Six powerful films that speak to all Christians about making the right choices, living adventurously, enjoying leisure without guilt, taking true godliness seriously, overcoming negative thinking, and establishing a biblical attitude toward authority. Available on video cassette and 16mm film.

MULTIPLE AUDIO CASSETTE PACKAGE

Living on the Ragged Edge. This series of 24 addresses on 12 audio cassettes draws a parallel between Solomon's story in Ecclesiastes and today's aggressive, success-oriented executive who attempts to find satisfaction in achievement alone.

SINGLE CASSETTES

Adolescents in Adult Bodies
Attitudes: Choosing the Food You Serve Your Mind
Dropping Your Guard
How to Enjoy Life . . . Now!
How to Stand Up When the World Is Pulling You Down
Improving Your Serve
Influence That Inspires
Kingdom Authority
Knowing God: Life's Major Pursuit
Needed: A Godly Mind
People of Refuge
Strategic Use of the Mind
Strengthening Your Grip on Money
Success: A Godly Perspective